LEARNING TO LEARN

STRENGTHENING STUDY SKILLS AND BRAIN POWER

Revised Edition

by
Gloria Frender

Incentive Publications, Inc.
Nashville, Tennessee

I hear and I forget;
I see and I remember;
I do and I understand
                    —Chinese Proverb

For Nylene and Clark, my parents . . . who gave me self-confidence and a love for learning
For Dean, Kevin, and Kim, my family . . . who continue to give me support and love

Designed by Marta Drayton
Cover by Janet March
Edited by Charlotte Bosarge

ISBN 978-0-86530-607-3

8   9   10   11   10

Printed by Sheridan Books, Inc., Chelsea, Michigan • November 2010
www.incentivepublications.com

Set a purpose.

Use active learning time wisely.

Concentrate only on one task at a time.

Commit yourself to learning.

Evaluate learning styles.

Schedule appropriate study times.

Summarize often.

Fully intend to remember.

Understand assignments.

List priorities.

Set realistic goals.

Think positively.

Use rewards.

Decide to become an independent learner.

You can use your learning style
to your advantage.

Survey textbooks
before reading.

Keep up with
daily assignments.

Improve your
memory mnemonics.

Listen actively in class.

Learn to organize everything.

Study successful test-taking strategies.

Table of Contents

NOTE-TAKING SKILLS

READING SKILLS

MEMORY

TEST-TAKING SKILLS

ETC.

Students of all abilities are often at risk when it comes to using successful learning strategies. Learning how to learn—applying successful techniques—is like mountain climbing with a backpack equipped with appropriate tools.

Throughout life we are always facing new and challenging mountains, and we depend upon the tools we carry with us to help us reach the top and attain our goals. It is vital for us to stock our backpacks with both the right background experiences and the tools to achieve a successful ascent. Most students forgo learning basic climbing skills or carefully gathering learning tools because they don't feel the need for them. But then, when the mountain finally looms before them, they often cannot begin to climb (much less scale) the peak. They are lost.

For many, the big mountain appears overwhelming and the climb hopeless. They begin to doubt their abilities, intelligence, and capabilities for learning.

Some potential climbers have natural ability and do not bother with extended practice, essential equipment, and critical experience. They may succeed for a while, but they usually become lost when they need this combination of resources the most. All too often, students find themselves suddenly facing the stressful predicament of acquiring *unfamiliar learning skills* and *content* simultaneously. They find themselves out on a ledge with no tools to help them.

Learning and practicing good, useful, and appropriate study skills builds self-confidence so that when faced with the challenge, students can successfully conquer their own mountains. It is vital they *learn how to learn* along with what they learn. Learning to learn is one of the most basic and important lifelong skills we can acquire. Our lives of learning are filled with hills and mountains. It's simply not enough to know what to climb; we must also know how to climb.

Learning to Learn is a book intended for students, teachers, parents, and anyone who wants a hands-on guide and reference for "learning how to learn." This book is not a book simply to read—it is a book to use, write in, and tear apart. It is an interactive book filled with practical hints, methods, tips, procedures, resources, and tools that will help students succeed in school and in life. Care has been taken to omit any "educational jargon" and to present the material in a straightforward manner.

The format of organized step-by-step procedures has been broken down into manageable blocks that can apply across the content areas. Throughout the book, the main concepts are stressed with a positive attitude, a feeling of accomplishment and self-worth, and a sense of humor. Good ideas are easy to find, digest, and put to immediate use.

Begin today to fill those backpacks with terrific lifelong learning skills and climb any "learning mountain" with confidence!

LEARNING STYLES

FOCUS ON

*L*EARNING *S*TYLES

1. Know how you learn.

2. Combine HOW and WHY with WHAT you learn.

3. Be aware of the time and environment where you learn best.

4. Apply various learning activities to meet your needs.

5. Utilize all your senses in learning something.

6. Apply how you learn to all new situations.

7. Be flexible in your thinking and learning.

8. Intentionally decide which learning modality to use.

9. Analyze your teacher's teaching style and apply appropriate learning strategies.

10. Creatively adapt materials to best fit your personal learning strengths.

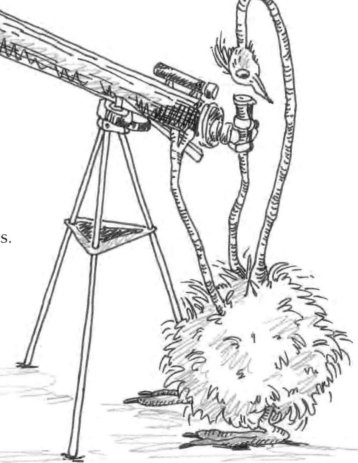

You are what you are! Each individual naturally functions and learns in a particular manner. Although your brain usually functions as a "whole," it actually is divided into two hemispheres. Both hemispheres act and react, think and process, and solve problems in very specific ways. Each is quite different from the other, and one is usually dominant. The best "brain power" is a result of both hemispheres integrating with almost equal balance.

You learn primarily through three basic modalities which use your senses: visual (seeing), auditory (hearing), and kinesthetic (feeling and doing). Just like left or right hemisphere brain dominance, one of the three modalities is usually dominant.

In order to "learn how to learn," it is very important to learn how you presently take in and process information. Knowing the strengths and weaknesses of your individual learning style will allow you to make adjustments so that you may reach your fullest potential in whatever you wish to do or learn. Assessing your learning style is the first step toward achieving maximum use of your "brain power." Learning to assess other other people's teaching style will enable you to make adjustments in your learning styles. This allows you to learn from any teacher!

Self-assessments in the areas of brain ability and modality strengths, as well as specific attributes of each, may be found on pages 17-26. This information will be invaluable to you as you continue your journey toward more effective and efficient learning.

Read the following statements and circle the numbers of statements that describe you. Make quick decisions and trust your first responses. The scoring table at the end of the list will help you determine your "dominance." You may find that you are fairly balanced between the two hemispheres.

1. I have no trouble making decisions about the correct thing to do.

2. I see problems or pictures as a whole rather than in parts or details.

3. I follow written directions best and prefer to write and talk.

4. I often think of many things at once rather than thinking through one idea at a time.

5. I'm usually aware of the time.

6. When I'm introduced to someone for the first time, I pay particular attention to the person's face. I later forget the person's name, but I remember his or her face.

7. I attack most problem-solving activities analytically and logically.

8. When comparing things, I usually look for ways they are alike rather than ways they are different.

9. I'd rather take a true/false, multiple-choice, or matching test than an essay test.

10. Most often, I use my imagination and think in an abstract manner.

11. If I have a problem, I break it down into smaller, more manageable parts in order to arrive at a solution.

12. I seem to learn best if I can observe a demonstration or read the directions.

13. Generally, I like to be in control of a situation and I do not like to take too many risks.

14. I like assignments that are open-ended rather than more structured assignments.

15. I learn best by seeing and hearing.

16. I learn best by touching or doing.

17. I usually think in concrete patterns and solve problems with a step-by-step approach.

18. If I try to remember information, I generally picture it in my mind.

19. Although I sometimes get upset, I am a rational person.

20. I don't mind trying anything once; I take risks when it is necessary.

21. Sometimes I talk to myself in order to think or learn something.

22. I can let my feelings "go." I am considered to be somewhat emotional.

23. I solve problems on an intellectual basis rather than an intuitive one.

24. People have told me that I'm creative.

25. I prefer to plan things and to know what's going to happen ahead of time.

26. I like to act in a spontaneous manner.

27. I prefer to think of one thing at a time.

28. I can easily remember melodies and tunes.

29. I am usually in control of my feelings.

30. I do well in geometry and geography.

31. I usually can recall information I need quickly and easily.

32. I enjoy reading and writing poetry; it comes to me easily.

33. I can really concentrate when I want to.

34. When I work in a group, I can "feel" the moods of others.

35. I understand mathematical concepts.

36. When solving problems or taking tests, I rely on one idea leading to another in order to come to a conclusion.

37. I can learn new vocabulary words easily.

38. When I plan a party, I "hang loose" rather than plan all of the details.

39. I usually can learn easily from any teacher.

40. In class I'm generally aware of what everyone is doing.

41. I notice and remember details.

42. I can easily see the whole picture when only a few puzzle pieces are in place.

43. I don't mind practicing something repeatedly in order to master it.

44. I communicate best with someone "in person" rather than on the phone.

45. I can remember jokes and punch lines.

46. I have trouble concentrating when I know I should.

47. I can write directions in a clear and logical manner.

48. I sometimes rely on my intuition when making decisions.

49. I basically have a day-to-day routine.

50. I sometimes can remember things according to where I "saw" them on the page.

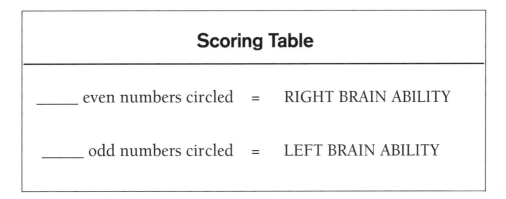

Scoring Table

_____ even numbers circled = RIGHT BRAIN ABILITY

_____ odd numbers circled = LEFT BRAIN ABILITY

Remember, this inventory is only an informal indication of which hemisphere is probably dominant for you. Both sides work together and cannot be totally separated.

LEFT

- sequential
- intellectual
- structured/planned
- controls feelings
- analytical
- logical
- remembers names
- rational
- solves problems by breaking them apart
- time-oriented
- auditory/visual learner
- prefers to write and talk
- follows spoken directions
- talks to think and learn
- prefers T/F, multiple-choice and matching tests
- takes few risks (with control)
- looks for the differences
- controls right side of body
- thinks mathematically
- thinks concretely
- language abilities
- thinks of one thing at a time

RIGHT

- holistic
- intuitive
- spontaneous
- lets feelings go
- creative/responsive
- more abstract
- remembers faces
- more likely to act on emotions
- solves problems by looking at the whole
- spatially oriented
- kinesthetic learner
- prefers to draw and handle objects
- follows written or demonstrated directions
- "pictures" things to think and learn
- prefers essay tests
- takes more risks (less control)
- looks for similar qualities
- controls left side of body
- musical abilities
- emotional
- thinks simultaneously

Use these activities to encourage the success of left/right brain dominant learners. Integrating both hemispheres increases learning potential and more effective use of your brain.

LEFT	RIGHT
• break down concepts into smaller, sequential parts or steps	• discuss, draw, write the major concept first before learning it
• use concrete examples to make abstract concepts more understandable	• encourage use of imagination through creative writing, dramatics, story telling
• encourage logical step-by-step problem-solving techniques	• discuss the role of feelings in decision making
• discuss the role of organized concrete thinking in decision making	• use role-playing activities
• learn various strategies to analyze specific problems	• use creative craft materials for inventive projects
• recognize, appreciate, and understand solution steps in logical thinking	• use graphic organizers to illustrate the "whole" concept
• use games, toys, materials with specific conclusions and purposes	• use manipulative materials to provide "hands-on" orientation that demonstrates spatial relationships
• break down major concepts into contributing parts; organize these parts into sub-groups	• use touch and movement activities
• use materials that help organize (binders, daily planners, calendars)	• use illustrations whenever possible; "when in doubt, draw it out"
• use graphic organizers to illustrate the parts or steps combined to achieve the whole concept	• conduct experiments
• use manipulative materials that demonstrate a process	• apply brainstorming strategies
• discuss or repeat orally while writing	• use written instructions and have students create their own
• use written and oral instructions (teachers) and repeat them back orally (students)	• demonstrate how to build or make something
• talk aloud while studying when appropriate	• make collage pictures
• discuss specific facts and details	• utilize "open-ended" discussions to examine all sides of a problem/answer
• organize brainstorming ideas into a conclusion	• use "open-ended" games, puzzles, etc.
• play games that minimize risk taking	• play games that encourage risk taking
• play games or use problem solving strategies that encourage finding varying/different attributes or characteristics	• play games or use problem solving strategies that encourage finding common attributes or characteristics
• encourage involvement in mathematical and various scientific activities	• encourage involvement in a wide variety of musical activities
• encourage talking through problems	• discuss appropriate and acceptable outlets for emotions
• use or create humor	• use problem-solving strategies that encourage simultaneous thinking
	• observe completion of tasks before trying it independently
	• encourage students to create their own problem-solving systems
	• use abstract materials
	• encourage self-improvement rather than peer competition
	• devise methods to help with organizational skills; make lists, use calendars, assignment sheets
	• use spelling aids, visual memory strategies
	• use or create humor

A learning modality is a way of using sensory information to learn. Basically, there are three modalities you use to process material into your memory. They are as follows:

- visual — learn from seeing
- auditory — learn from hearing
- kinesthetic — learn from touching, doing, moving

As stated before, almost every individual has one dominant modality. However, many people have a "balance" between two or even all three modalities. It is very important to know your primary mode of learning so that you will know how to approach learning and how to apply certain methods that will aid you the most.

First, complete the self-assessment on pages 23–25 to find out what your strongest modality is. Then, refer to the chart of Suggested Aids for Learning Modalities on page 27 for specific hints and methods you can use to increase your learning power.

Read each question or statement and circle the most appropriate answer. Some will be difficult to answer, but try to respond according to how you would react most often.

1. You usually remember more from a class lecture when:
    a. you do not take notes but listen very closely
    b. you sit near the front of the room and watch the speaker
    c. you take notes (whether or not you look at them again)

2. You usually solve problems by:
    a. talking to yourself or a friend
    b. using an organized, systematic approach with lists, schedules, etc.
    c. walking, pacing, or some other physical activity

3. You remember phone numbers (when you can't write them down) by:
    a. repeating the numbers orally
    b. "seeing" or "visualizing" the numbers in your mind
    c. "writing" the numbers with your finger on a table or wall

4. You find it easiest to learn something new by:
    a. listening to someone explain how to do it
    b. watching a demonstration of how to do it
    c. trying it yourself

5. You remember most clearly from a movie:
    a. what the characters said, background noises, and music
    b. the setting, scenery, and costumes
    c. the feelings you experienced during the movie

6. When you go to the grocery store, you:
    a. silently or orally repeat the grocery list
    b. walk up and down the aisles to see what you need
    c. usually remember what you need from the list you left at home

7. You are trying to remember something, so you:

    a. hear in your mind what was said or the noises that occurred

    b. try to see it happen in your mind

    c. feel the way "it" affected your emotions

8. You learn a foreign language best by:

    a. listening to records or tapes

    b. writing and using workbooks

    c. attending a class in which you read and write the language

9. You are confused about the correct spelling of a word, so you:

    a. sound it out

    b. try to "see" the word in your mind

    c. write the word several different ways and choose the one that looks right

10. You enjoy reading most when you can read:

    a. dialogue between characters

    b. descriptive passages that allow you to create mental pictures

    c. stories with a lot of action in the beginning (because you have a hard time sitting still)

11. You usually remember people you have met by their:

    a. names (you forget faces)

    b. faces (you forget names)

    c. mannerisms, motions, etc.

12. You are distracted most by:

    a. noises

    b. people

    c. environment (temperature, comfort of furniture, etc.)

13. You usually dress:
   a. fairly well (but clothes are not very important to you)
   b. neatly (in a particular style)
   c. comfortably (so you can move easily)

14. You can't do anything physical and you can't read, so you choose to:
   a. talk with a friend
   b. watch TV or look out a window
   c. move slightly in your chair or bed

Scoring Table

1. Count the total number of responses for each letter and write them below.

   a. _____ auditory   (learn best by hearing)

   b. _____ visual   (learn best by seeing)

   c. _____ kinesthetic   (learn best by touching, doing, moving)

2. Notice if one modality is significantly higher or lower, or if any two modalities are close in number (two point difference).

3. Were the results as you expected them to be? Is that the way you see yourself? How do you see others?

CHARACTERISTICS OF LEARNING STYLES

Three of your five senses are used primarily in learning, storing, remembering, and recalling information. Your eyes, ears, and sense of touch play essential roles in the way you communicate, perceive reality, and relate to others. Because you learn from and communicate best with someone who shares your dominant modality, it is a great advantage for you to know the characteristics of visual, auditory, and kinesthetic learning styles and to be able to identify them in others.

VISUAL	AUDITORY	KINESTHETIC
• mind sometimes strays during verbal activities	• talks to self aloud	• likes physical rewards
• observes rather than talks or acts	• enjoys talking	• in motion most of the time
• organized in approach to tasks	• easily distracted	• likes to touch people when talking to them
• likes to read	• has more difficulty with written directions	• taps pencil or foot while studying
• usually a good speller	• likes to be read to	• enjoys doing activities
• memorizes by seeing graphics and pictures	• memorizes by steps in a sequence	• reading is not a priority
• not too distractible	• enjoys music	• poor speller
• finds verbal instructions difficult	• whispers to self while reading	• likes to solve problems by physically working through them
• has good handwriting	• remembers faces	• will try new things
• remembers faces	• easily distracted by noises	• outgoing by nature; expresses emotions through physical means
• uses advanced planning	• hums or sings	• uses hands while talking
• doodles	• outgoing by nature	• dresses for comfort
• quiet by nature	• enjoys listening activities	• enjoys handling objects
• meticulous, neat in appearance		
• notices details		

Students who have equal modality preferences are more flexible learners and are already using many studying techniques rather than just a few.

Depending on which learning modality you determined was dominant for you, use these aids to sharpen your particular dominant learning modality or to strengthen a weaker one. Try to be aware of the different activities you do daily to develop all three of your modalities.

VISUAL	AUDITORY	KINESTHETIC
• use guided imagery	• use tapes	• pace or walk as you study
• form pictures in your mind	• watch TV	• physically "do it"
• take notes	• listen to music	• practice by repeated motion
• see parts of words	• speak and listen to speakers	• breathe slowly
• use "cue" words	• make up rhymes or poems	• role play
• use notebooks	• read aloud	• exercise
• use color coding	• talk to yourself	• dance
• use study/flash cards	• repeat things orally	• write
• use photographic pictures	• use rhythmic sounds	• write on surfaces with finger
• watch filmstrips	• have discussions	• take notes
• watch movies	• listen carefully	• associate feelings with concept/information
• use charts, graphs	• use oral directions	• write lists repeatedly
• use maps	• sound out words	• stretch and move in chair
• demonstrate	• use theater	• watch lips move in front of a mirror
• create and use drawings	• say words in syllables	• use mnemonics (word links, rhymes, poems, lyrics), refer to "Memory Chapter"
• use exhibits	• use mnemonics (word links, rhymes, poems, lyrics), refer to "Memory Chapter"	
• watch lips move in front of a mirror		
• use mnemonics (mind maps, visual chains, acronyms, acrostics, hook-ups), refer to "Memory Chapter"		

ELEMENTS FOR BETTER LEARNING

Be aware of all elements when you study and learn. Become knowledgeable about the characteristics of your learning style and apply them to create an effective learning environment. Increase focused concentration, efficient use of time, and brain power by considering the following important aspects:

Watch Your Environment

- Have the Right Attitude:
    - be motivated to learn
    - be persistent in pursuing short-term and long-term goals
    - keep a positive "CAN DO" attitude
    - accept responsibility for your own learning
    - vary working alone, with peers in a study group, and with mentors/tutors
    - apply your strengths of left/right brain dominance, auditory, visual, and kinesthetic learning modalities to everything you study
    - understand the need for organization and structure when you study

- Avoid Distractions:
    - watching or listening to TV
    - listening to music
    - sitting or lying on the bed
    - eating or drinking
    - using areas in traffic/active living areas of family members (kitchen, family/recreation room)
    - talking on the telephone
    - playing with unnecessary items on desk or table
    - positioning desk or table in front of windows

- Use the Right Tools:
    - a quiet study environment
    - a well-organized desk or study box stocked with appropriate supplies (see page 45)
    - appropriate lighting and room temperature to meet your needs
    - the best time of day when you feel the most motivated and able to concentrate
    - a scheduled routine of studying at the same time in the same place
    - a 10-minute active break time after each 30-minute study block

- Once you understand your learning style, you are more likely to know how to meet your own needs.

- Students can accurately predict their learning modalities.

- Students who are matched with teachers of the same learning style learn best. Students who can accurately predict their teachers' learning/teaching styles learn better than students who cannot make this prediction.

- A student's learning style is the same no matter what the subject area.

- Students score higher on tests when they are tested in the environments best suited to their personal learning styles—bright versus dim lighting, silence versus sound, etc.

- Persistent and responsible students achieve higher grades and score higher on tests.

- A key to quick learning and memory is to change the information to be learned into the form that the brain can learn most easily.

- The more a student can utilize learning through the combination of senses (visual, auditory, and kinesthetic modalities), the more permanent the information will become.

- Remember, to become an active learner:

HEAR IT
SEE IT
SAY IT
WRITE IT
DO IT

TIME MANAGEMENT & ORGANIZATION SKILLS

FOCUS ON
*T*IME *M*ANAGEMENT & *O*RGANIZATION

1. Intend to accomplish your goal in a reasonable amount of time.

2. Be realistic in eliminating excuses and reward yourself for positive behavior.

3. Break up long-term assignments into reasonable units.

4. Set priorities carefully in order to save time.

5. Organize your time, materials, and brain; keep them organized.

6. Use quality study time—not quantity study time.

7. Set realistic schedules and follow them.

8. Make time to warm up your mind and review your knowledge.

9. Make daily "To Do" lists.

10. Always ask yourself if that was the best use of your time.

11. Remember the results of your learning styles assessment. Choose time management and organization tools that focus on your strengths and minimize your weaknesses.

Time plays a major role in every enterprise on Earth. Time schedules form a foundation for every kind of work that is done.

Young people are naturally less conscious of time than people who have lived longer. During a child's early years, parents help to watch the clock and manage the child's time. The child begins to think of time as something invisible, controlled by his or her parents, regulating what he or she can do. As the child grows up and begins to think about gaining independence, he or she often imagines that this new freedom means no longer having to live by time rules.

The first and easiest way for a young person to gain more freedom is to prove his or her skill in handling time. When an individual can manage a time schedule successfully, without prodding or reminding from parents, he or she is well on the way to self-reliance. People learn to trust such an individual. Even more importantly, the individual learns to trust himself or herself.

Setting up a time schedule and making it work is something that requires commitment and perseverance. There are countless pitfalls in planning activities and assignments in terms of weeks, days, and hours. There are good reasons for "putting things off," and many mistakes often are made in determining how much actually can be done in a certain amount of time.

Discovering these problems is the first step toward progress—not a sign of failure. The second step is to revise your schedule to better fit your immediate need. Make this second revision more realistic, but set the goal a little beyond what you think will work. Again, this step will take more patience and persistence, but it will produce a more satisfactory system. The end result will be a more efficient and successful habit which subsequently gives you more time to spend as you wish!

As you review these time management techniques, focus on the elements that best fit your learning modality: visual, auditory, or kinesthetic.

A few suggested time management aids for the three modalities are:

VISUAL:	AUDITORY:	KINESTHETIC:
• Use "To Do" lists daily • Post reminder notes to yourself • Use color codes	• Use and give oral directions • Talk to yourself as a reminder • Make and use tapes	• Write on monthly calendars • Pace when you talk to yourself • Organize all study supplies within easy reach

From *The Campus Cache: A Cookbook For Study Skills*, the CMU Junior League, Cherry Creek School District, © 1982. Used by permission.

Just how well do you study? Have you thought seriously about how, when, where, and why you study? Knowing the answers to these questions can help you form some very important habits or improve the habits you already practice.

If you don't know the answers to these questions or you aren't sure if you're using time efficiently, perhaps some of these questions will help you think about what you need to do to improve.

Take a few minutes to complete the "Study Habits Inventory" (pages 36–38). You may find out some new things about yourself!

STUDY HABITS INVENTORY

	Hardly Ever	Sometimes	Most Always
1. Do you intend to study, concentrate, and learn?	_____	_____	_____
2. Do you follow a daily written schedule?	_____	_____	_____
3. Do you have a regular place to work and study?	_____	_____	_____
4. Is your study space well-equipped, well-lighted, and comfortable?	_____	_____	_____
5. Do you keep track of homework assignments in a book?	_____	_____	_____
6. Do you keep a long-term schedule or calendar of tests, projects, and reports?	_____	_____	_____
7. Do you plan weekly reviews?	_____	_____	_____
8. Do you take effective class notes?	_____	_____	_____
9. Do you keep a notebook for every subject?	_____	_____	_____
10. Are you organized?	_____	_____	_____
11. Do you have a note-taking system?	_____	_____	_____
12. Do you edit your notes?	_____	_____	_____
13. Do you compile study sheets for tests?	_____	_____	_____

From *Senior High Study Skills Booklet*, Jefferson County Schools, Colorado, © 1983. Used by permission.

	Hardly Ever	Sometimes	Most Always
14. Do you know how you learn best?	_____	_____	_____
15. Do you study with friends?	_____	_____	_____
16. Do you listen well in class?	_____	_____	_____
17. Do you know what distracts you?	_____	_____	_____
18. Do you look up new words?	_____	_____	_____
19. Do you keep track of new words you learn?	_____	_____	_____
20. Do you use the glossary?	_____	_____	_____
21. Do you have a study system for textbooks?	_____	_____	_____
22. Do you outline reading assignments?	_____	_____	_____
23. Do you skim assignments before reading them?	_____	_____	_____
24. Do you read tables, charts, and graphs?	_____	_____	_____
25. Do you have a private shorthand system for taking notes?	_____	_____	_____
26. Do you organize papers before you write?	_____	_____	_____

From *Senior High Study Skills Booklet*,
Jefferson County Schools, Colorado, © 1983. Used by permission.

	Hardly Ever	Sometimes	Most Always
27. Do you write a first draft?	_____	_____	_____
28. Do you proofread for spelling and punctuation errors?	_____	_____	_____
29. Do you study effectively?	_____	_____	_____
30. Do you learn in school?	_____	_____	_____
31. Do you get enough sleep every night?	_____	_____	_____
32. Do you exercise regularly?	_____	_____	_____
33. Do you study at the same time each day?	_____	_____	_____
34. Do you make good use of your mind?	_____	_____	_____
35. Do you try to improve your study habits?	_____	_____	_____
36. Do you space your study periods over several days?	_____	_____	_____
37. Do you keep up-to-date with your studies?	_____	_____	_____
38. Do you review often?	_____	_____	_____

If you find yourself saying these things, then perhaps you'd better ask yourself these questions:

"I'm here and that's enough."
> **Ask yourself** "Since I'm not putting out any effort, should I expect anything in return?"

"I just don't have the time."
> **Ask yourself** "Is studying really a priority? How many things do I find to do that don't have to be done, at least right now?"

"Well, I'll start tomorrow."
> **Ask yourself** "How many times have I said that? Is that a convenient excuse? What will I say tomorrow?"

"I can't!"
> **Ask yourself** "How many different ways or methods have I tried? How many times have I tried? Have I tried to get help?"

"I don't need to study."
> **Ask yourself** "Why do I think this? What is my grade in the class?"

"I'm just too tired."
> **Ask yourself** "Would I be this tired if I had the choice to do something else? How much sleep did I get last night?"

"It's boring."
> **Ask yourself** "What do I expect to get out of this? How have I tried to relate the information to my life? Do I really need the information?"

"It's just too much for me, so why start now?"
> **Ask yourself** "Is there anything I can realistically accomplish now? Why am I in this mess? When should I have started the assignment?"

Now, tell yourself

"I WILL . . . AND I CAN!"

Remember the 10-second rule: If you can't find what you are looking for in 10 seconds you lose your focus. Following are the places you must make sure are organized if you are to study and learn effectively:

LOCKER

- Use shelves to best divide available space.
- Use magnetic boxes, etc. inside locker door for quick access to supplies.
- Use Post-it® Notes to write reminders to be taken with you.
- Use a small magnetic dry-erase board to write more permanent notes and ideas.

BACKPACK

- Use for transport, not storage.
- Use special pockets designed for specific items.
- Lighten the load:
    - Schedule a 5-minute period each week to clean and reorganize.
    - Keep minimal notebooks, binders, texts, extra paper, and supplies.

BINDER (current papers only)

- Why a 3-ring binder is best:
    - Allows for easy addition and/or deletion of papers
    - Allows for rearrangement of papers
    - Keeps papers securely
    - Allows for color-coded, tabbed section dividers
    - Provides storage for needed supplies (see *Handy Supply Checklist* on page 44)
- Write your name, street, phone number, and email address in a prominent location.
- Use a 3-hole plastic/cloth pouch in each binder for general supplies.
    - Consider class subjects in binder when selecting supplies.
- Use assignment sheets:
    - Keep 5–10 blank sheets in a pocket of the binder you use first each day.
    - Begin with a new assignment sheet each day.
    - Combine all your classes on one sheet.
- Use a portable 3-hole punch for handouts:
    - Immediately use it if necessary for handouts/loose papers.
    - Place handout in correct section of notebook to avoid losing papers.

- Use colored divider pages:
  - Assign a different color for each subject (see *The Wonders of Color Coding* on page 46). Example: green for science, blue for language arts, etc.
  - Place clear tabs behind each colored tab divider and label them:
    - Class notes
    - Handouts
    - Homework
    - Add any extras as needed: lab (science), writing projects (language arts), maps (geography), etc.
  - Consider special, labeled sections for:
    - Class requirements/rules
    - Monthly calendars
    - Lists of classmates and phone/email information
    - Extra notebook paper

DESK TOP

- Use a good lamp, positioned below eye level and focused on reading material
- Place computer to one side to allow room to study
- Use a pencil/pen holder.
  - Regularly discard used pens and replenish lead/erasers in mechanical pencils
- Use a 4-section paper tray for quick, easy access to:
  - Notebook paper
  - Scratch paper
  - Unlined paper
  - Special paper (graph, colored, construction, etc.)
- Create a reference section (on desk top with bookends, or a shelf easily accessible from chair).
  - Dictionary (thumb-hole format)
  - Thesaurus (dictionary format with thumb holes)
  - General reference book
    - Highly recommended: *Write Source,* Houghton Mifflin Company; *Writers Inc., A Student Handbook for Writing and Learning,* Sebranek/Kemper/Meyer
  - Specific subject area materials
    - Atlas, almanac
    - Quick academic guides (usually plastic-coated folders)

DESK DRAWERS

- Use drawer divider trays whenever possible
  - Stock with appropriate supplies (see *Handy Supply Checklist* on page 44).
- Create a home filing system (file drawer/separate box of completed units for future use: review for midterm/final exams).
  - Use one labeled, colored folder per subject (see *The Wonders of Color Coding* on page 46).
    - ▲ Use the same colors you used for your notebook dividers, flash cards (see *The Magic of Flash Cards* on page 112).
      Example: green for science, blue for language arts, etc.
  - Clip together all class notes, quizzes/tests, handouts, homework, etc. into a packet.
    - ▲ Clean out your binder and backpack for all related papers.
  - Label this packet with specific topic, text chapter/unit, pages, etc.
  - File immediately in the correct folder when completing a unit of study.

WHY USE A HOME FILING SYSTEM?

- Establishes one place to organize past units of study
- Keeps all papers together according to unit
- Provides easy future access to review materials for midterm/final exams
- Keeps all assignments. If your teacher mistakenly gives you an incorrect grade or is missing an assignment in the grade book:
  - It is your responsibility to show the corrected assignment to the teacher.
  - You can find any assignments for which you did not get credit.
  - If you can find it, you can prove you did it and can get credit for it.
- Keeps all papers until you have checked your report card and permanent transcript to make sure you received the proper credit and grade. If not, you now have organized proof on your side.
- Provides a separate file for you in which to keep your major work:
  - Major reports, writing papers, etc. to rework for later assignments if necessary (Jr./Sr. high students heading to college). It's better than starting over from scratch!
    - ▲ You will have to rewrite these assignments to better fit the new assignment and you will have improved your writing skills from the original paper.

 ©Incentive Publications, Inc., Nashville, TN

How to Organize Anything

THIS METHOD:

- Saves time
- Helps make quick decisions
- Provides immediate success
- Limits focus on one task/area at a time
- Works for any area: closet, desk top, drawers, cabinets, shelves, etc.

STEP 1 ☞ Label three containers (each should be size-appropriate to items in closet, desk, etc.): (1) *"Desk"*
(2) *"Trash"*
(3) *"Elsewhere"*

STEP 2 ☞ Place each item in the correct container as you remove it from the area you are organizing

STEP 3 ☞ Replace all items in container labeled "Desk" (closet, drawer, etc.) after completely clearing and cleaning the space

STEP 4 ☞ Take the "Trash" container and empty it into the trash

STEP 5 ☞ Take the "Elsewhere" container and put all items where they belong (in different areas in your room or around the house, garage, etc.)

Remember:

PUT IN ONE PLACE—LOOK IN ONE PLACE.

ONCE ORGANIZED—STAY ORGANIZED.

- *Schedule five minutes one day a week* to clean, reorganize, and update:
  - Desk top
    - Paper holder
    - Pen/pencil container
    - Reference section
  - Desk drawers
    - Replenish needed supplies
  - Backpack
  - Flash card file
  - Home filing system
    - Remove all papers that are not currently being used
  - Large calendar posted in your room
  - Locker
- *Use generic headings* to save time when labeling notebook section dividers, home filing system folders, flash card tabs, etc.

HANDY SUPPLY CHECKLIST

LOCKER

____ Sturdy shelves (2)

____ Magnetic boxes to hold extra supplies (pens, mechanical pencils, etc.)

____ Magnetic Post-it® Notes (or purchase regular Post-it® Notes and a magnet strip to glue on the back)

____ Small magnetic dry-erase board (measure locker door first)

____ Dry-erase pens

____ Facial tissue

____ Specific containers for computer disks, etc. if desired

BACKPACK

____ Sturdy fabric (check out the bottom and shoulder straps)

____ Padded, adjustable shoulder straps

____ Good zippers

____ Separate compartments/pockets (not just one big one)

____ Sub-divider pockets within compartments

____ Easy access to all compartments/pockets

BINDERS

____ Sturdy 1–2" size

____ Pockets on inside and back covers

BINDER SUPPLIES

____ Plastic/fabric pouch for each binder

____ Large enough for appropriate supplies

____ Separate pockets for computer discs, pens/pencils, etc.

____ Colored, tabbed dividers

____ Same colors as you assigned for each subject (see *The Wonders of Color Coding* on page 46)

____ Clear, tabbed dividers

____ Enough for minimum of three per subject

____ Plastic 3-hole punch for handouts

____ Folder for notebook paper and new assignment sheets

REFERENCE SECTION SUPPLIES

____ Dictionary

____ Thesaurus

____ Student Handbook

____ Quick Reference Academic Guides (specific subject areas)

____ Almanac

____ Atlas

©Incentive Publications, Inc., Nashville, TN

DESK SUPPLIES

___ Lamp

___ Pen/pencil holder

___ Pens, mechanical pencils, extra lead, extra erasers

___ Water soluble transparency pens (for large calendars)

___ Colored highlighters

___ Colored pencils

___ Paper divider trays

___ Notebook paper

___ Computer paper (or any paper without lines)

___ Special paper (graph, colored construction, map, etc.)

___ Bookends (if appropriate) for reference books

___ Colored file folders for home filing system file drawer

___ Extra file folder for new assignment sheets, monthly binder calendars, reports in progress, etc.

___ Drawer divider organizers for:

    ___ Rubber bands

    ___ White out

    ___ Rubber cement

    ___ Ruler

    ___ Compass

    ___ Protractor

    ___ Tape

    ___ Scissors

___ Box, if desired, for home filing system

___ Timer (to time 30-minute study blocks (see *Rules for Study Time: The Backbone of Success* on page 65)

___ Stapler

___ Staples

___ Staple remover

___ Paper clips

___ Binder clips (for large stacks of papers)

___ Push pins for bulletin board

___ Calculator, extra batteries if needed

___ Templates if desired (see *Creating A Graphic Organizer* on page 119)

___ Colored 3" x 5" index cards

___ Split rings (see *The Magic of Flash Cards* on page 112)

___ Storage box for 3" x 5" cards

___ Colored tabs to label 3" x 5" card section dividers (see *The Magic of Flash Cards* on page 112)

___ Post-it® Notes

MISCELLANEOUS

___ Computer

___ Bulletin board

___ Facial tissue

___ Large monthly calendar (or two) (see *Use a Monthly Calendar* on page 56)

___ Cassette recorder (practicing speeches, foreign language, vocabulary review)

THE WONDERS OF COLOR CODING

Colors are the most important, most easily recognized, and longest-remembered asset to learning—so why not use them to your studying advantage every chance you get? Think about using color in everything you do:

- to organize materials/supplies in your locker, backpack, desk, binder, large wall monthly calendars, and binder calendars
- to organize subject information including main topics, sub-topics, details, and examples in notes, study sheets, and graphic organizers
- to organize your closet and storage areas with colored labels, containers, hangers, etc.
- to organize your address book using colored highlighters to signify different groups of people (school friends, relatives, work/job contacts, businesses, etc.)

Color Coding for School

STEP 1 ☞ List on a sheet of paper all school subjects that require homework.

STEP 2 ☞ Assign a different color to each subject using red, blue, green, yellow, orange, purple.
- Example: science—green, language arts—yellow

STEP 3 ☞ Binder
- Label each colored tab with generic topics for reuse year after year.
  - Example: "Math", not algebra
- Place and label three clear, tabbed pages behind each colored tab:
  - Class notes
  - Handouts
  - Homework

STEP 4 ☞ Home Filing System
- Label appropriate colored file folders, one per subject.
- Use generic headings.
- Keep in file drawer, cabinet, or box.

STEP 5 ☞ Textbooks
- Cover all textbooks.
- Using the appropriate colored marker, make a large dot on the spine and front of each book. This allows you to find the correct book quickly when your books are stacked in your locker or on your home desk.
- Never grab the wrong book again!

STEP 6 ☞ Notes to Yourself
- Use different-colored Post-it® Notes to help you remember things during the day.
- Example: yellow—school, pink—home, green—activities

Remember, teachers vary in the way they give assignments. Do not depend on them to tell you to write the assignment down—this is your responsibility.

A Daily Assignment Sheet Will . . .

- . . . keep you organized by establishing one central place to write down assignments
- . . . end frustrations from having to look in numerous places or losing many scraps of paper
- . . . keep you on track every day
- . . . lower stress about forgetting
- . . . reinforce completion of assignments/tasks
- . . . provide clear, concise, written information for later application (you won't be confused during your study time after a long day of classes and many assignments)
- . . . provide easy, organized reference to transfer information to large monthly home calendar
- . . . provide an appropriate space to immediately write down exams and assignments due later so you won't forget to plan for them

Listen and Look for Assignments

- Listen carefully for assignments to be given.
- Do not depend on a teacher to specifically say, "Your assignment for tomorrow is . . .". Some teachers have a less direct approach in giving oral assignments.
- Be alert for a specific time of class your teacher gives assignments; know the routine for every class.
- Always check the dry-erase/chalk board, bulletin board, large class calendar or anywhere else teachers post assignments every class period.
- Make it a habit to double-check your written assignment for accuracy before you leave class.
- Mentally link closing your binder at the end of each class with writing down the assignment.

Write Down ALL Assignments ALL the Time

- Use a new assignment sheet every day.
- Write on only one side so nothing will get lost or missed on the back side.
- Immediately, when assignments are given, take out your assignment sheet and fill in all the appropriate columns.
- Use the columns to your advantage; they remind you of needed information.

ASSIGNMENT COLUMN

Write in the actual assignment.
Example: math p 155 all odd, sci read pp 132–9/take notes, hist p 147 quest. 1–7

DUE DATE COLUMN

Write in the appropriate date when the assignment is to be turned in.
Example: 11/6

ESTIMATED TIME COLUMN

Write in the estimated time it will take you to complete this assignment. (This will help you better use your time efficiently and effectively.)
Example: 30 min.

Use these steps when you first begin your assignment in class or home study time:

STEP 1 ☞ Time yourself while completing one problem, reading one page, answering one question.

STEP 2 ☞ Multiply by the number of problems, pages, or questions to be done.

STEP 3 ☞ Add five minutes (just to be on the safe side).

STEP 4 ☞ You now have a good estimate of how long it will take you to complete this assignment.

If your teacher states an appropriate amount of time he thinks it should take to complete the assignment, write it down and circle it. This way, you can see how it will compare to your written estimate and you won't forget it.

MATERIALS NEEDED COLUMN

Write in the materials you will need to take home with you so you won't forget them or take home the wrong ones.

● Use of this column will save you time and stress later at home, as it helps insure that you will have the necessary materials on hand.

● Use these abbreviations to save time:
  ■ T—textbook
  ■ H—handout
  ■ P—packet
  ■ L—lab sheet

DONE COLUMN

Check off the column when assignments have been completed and placed in the correct section of your binder (see *Organize Your Materials!* on page 41). It will make you feel GREAT!

THIS WEEK, LATER, AND EXAMS SECTIONS

THIS WEEK: In this section write every assignment due tomorrow for all classes.

LATER: In this section write all assignments due beyond tomorrow.

Example: two days to a month

EXAMS: Write all exams coming up—tomorrow or in the future. Remember that even if a teacher does not give a specific date for an upcoming exam, but says ". . . next week there will be a test . . .", write it down anyway. You can begin to plan ahead and study ahead—today.

Hints: • *Place a few assignment sheets in each of your binders and use a new one each day.*

• *Place several assignments sheets in a labeled file folder in your desk to replenish your binder supply as needed (check this once a week).*

• *At the beginning of your home study time (see <u>Rules for Study Time: The Backbone of Success</u> on page 65) write down on your lar ge monthly home calendar all assignments /exams from the Later /Exams column on your assignment sheet (see <u>Assignment Sheet</u> on page 51) and any written on <u>Monthly Assignment Calendar</u> (see page 60).*

• *If your school requires you to use a specific daytimer or you prefer to use a daytimer book, consider making additional columns or spaces.*

Having Trouble Remembering To Write Down Assignments? Try These:

● Put a special key chain or tag on the zipper pull of your backpack compartment where you put your class binder and textbook. Every time you see this at the end of each class, it will remind you to write down the assignment.

● Place a brightly colored Post-it® Note on the front of your binder with "ASSIGNMENT?" clearly written on it. Each time you close your binder before putting it into your backpack you will see it.

● Use your dry-erase board in your locker to write yourself a daily reminder so you will see it each time you open your locker.

☑ Skim the entire assignment.
"Do I have an overall idea of what is to be completed?"

☑ Relate previous knowledge.
"What do I already know about this?"

☑ Read the directions twice.
"Do I really understand what is being asked or what I am supposed to do?"

☑ Decide the purpose of the assignment.
"What am I supposed to learn?
How and why is this useful information?"

☑ Decide the outcome.
"What should be the final product?
What will be the format?"

☑ Decide on and adapt the appropriate learning modality.
"What kind of audio, visual, or kinesthetic strategies are asked for?
Is this a left- or right-brain activity?
How can I adapt my dominant learning strategy to the assignment?"

☑ Choose mnemonic device(s).
"What is the best strategy to apply in order to memorize this material?"

☑ Gather needed materials.
"What materials do I need to complete this assignment?"

☑ Determine the sequence.
"Where should I begin?
What's the best sequence?"

☑ Do the assignment.
"Do I intend to learn this information?"

☑ Review.
"Could I teach this to someone else?"

	Assignment	Due Date	Estimated Time	Materials Needed	Done
THIS WEEK					
LATER					

WEEK OF _____

	MATERIAL TESTED	TEST DATE	TYPE OF TEST	SPECIAL NOTES
EXAMS				

WHAT TO DO IF YOU MISSED AN ASSIGNMENT

START → Did you do your homework?

Did you do your homework?
- NO → Can you get assignment from a friend?
- YES → Did you turn it in?

Can you get assignment from a friend?
- NO → Does your teacher post assignments?
- YES → Get it!

Does your teacher post assignments?
- NO → Will you ask for it from your teacher?
- YES → Get it!

Will you ask for it from your teacher?
- NO → Do you care if you get it in?
- YES → Get it!

Do you care if you get it in?
- YES → (back to) Can you get assignment from a friend?
- NO → Dead End!

Dead End! → Your grade is zero!

Get it! → (back to) Did you do your homework?

Did you turn it in?
- YES → Great! You completed it– Good Job!
- NO → You did it for nothing

Great! You completed it– Good Job! → **END!**

You did it for nothing → Your grade is zero!

From *The Campus Cache: A Cookbook For Study Skills*, the CMU Junior League,
Cherry Creek School District, © 1982. Used by permission.

Want more freedom to manage your own time? Want more free time? Use this highly successful system! For every five minutes you spend planning, you save twenty minutes of frustration some time within that day! A "To Do" list is a daily, written, prioritized list of tasks and activities to help organize your day.

Why Make a "To Do" List Every Day?

- Your mind constantly seeks your daily goals and a plan to reach them
- Once you write down your daily goals it eases your mind and reduces stress
- You can control your day and activities by planning ahead
- You can make more and better choices
- You will have more time to act (not react) to things that happen throughout the day
- You create your focus and prioritize your goals
- It is the most important three to five minutes you'll spend in organizing your day
- You are 10 times more likely to remember something if you write it down
- For each task you need to do, you reward yourself with an activity you want to do
- You feel a sense of accomplishment when you complete a task and cross it off

Follow These Steps to Success

STEP 1　☞　While you brush your teeth each night, think of three things you need to do and three things you want to do tomorrow.

STEP 2　☞　After brushing your teeth, immediately use a 3" x 5" card to briefly write these ideas in the appropriate sections using the model below.

- Use one to two words for each activity
- These must be realistic and important activities (do not include going to school, coming home, eating, or trivial, unimportant activities)
- *Good examples:* returning library book, studying, getting missed assignment due to sick day, doing dishes, emptying trash, etc.

STEP 3 🖝 Write the letters "M" or "A" or "N" in front of each bullet to prioritize your day:

- Use "M" for morning activities
  (any task to be done between the time you get up and lunch)

- Use "A" for afternoon activities
  (any task to be done between lunch and dinner)

- Use "N" for night activities
  (any task to be done between dinner and bedtime)

STEP 4 🖝 Combine the columns into one list at the bottom of the card:

- Take the "M" item from the "Need To Do" column and write it as #1.

- Take the "M" item from the "Want To Do" column and write it as #2.

- Repeat the two steps above for the "A" and "N" items.

- Remember, every day will be different:

  - You may not have any "M" items; if not, begin your list with the first "A" item.

  - Your columns may not have an even distribution of "Need" and "Want" items that match perfectly so use the rule that you must first choose an item from the "Need" column then reward yourself, if possible, with an item from the "Want" column.

  - Your columns may have more than one "M" or "A" or "N", so prioritize within the time block (what needs to be done first, second, third in the afternoon).

  - Use your common sense when creating your list.

STEP 5 🖝 Review the final list and ask yourself if it is realistic.

STEP 6 🖝 Add to your list as things come up during the day by writing these activities in the appropriate prioritized space.

STEP 7 🖝 If one task from your list does not get completed, add it to the next day's list if appropriate.

STEP 8   ☞ If the same task appears on your list for more than three days in a row, consider:

- . . . how important it is to do NOW—then move it to #1 on tomorrow's list.

- . . . writing it on a separate 3″ x 5″ card and putting it in a file for later.

- . . . dropping it completely.

Points to Consider

- Keep this list with you in your pocket, binder, or backpack.
- Be realistic—there are only 24 hours in each day.
- Cross off items as you do them (this gives you immediate satisfaction and it measures and shows your progress).
- Ask yourself these questions when setting priorities: "What must be done by tomorrow?" and "How can I best use my time at this point in the day?"
- Use index cards or a small notebook.
- Estimate (realistically) the amount of time needed to complete each task.
- Give yourself a reward at the end of the day for successfully completing each task on your list.

SAMPLE: "TO DO" LIST

NEED	WANT
A return book	N read book
M get sci. assign.	A shoot baskets
N study time	A play comp. game
1. Get sci. assign.	
2. Return book	
3. Shoot baskets	
4. Play comp. game	
5. Study Time	
6. Read book	

Using a monthly calendar helps you to make a commitment to planning ahead. It also helps you to see the whole picture of many weeks at one time and physically shows sequential steps necessary to complete a project/assignment on time.

MAKE A LARGE GENERIC CALENDAR

● With a full piece of poster board:

   ■ Use a wide, black felt marker and yardstick to mark off squares large enough to include several written activities/tasks.

   ■ Include all seven days of the week and a total of five weeks. At the top of each column label the days of the week, leaving a blank space for the month name.

   ■ Cover the entire calendar with matte (dull) translucent contact paper, or buy large, laminated, one- and two-month calendars from office supply stores.

   ■ Use a black water-soluble transparency pen to fill in the correct numbered days and the name of the month.

   ■ Use colored water-soluble transparency pens to write in all assignments. Match each color with the appropriate subject—the same ones you use for your notebooks (see *The Wonders of Color Coding* on page 46).

● Use two (or even three) calendars when assignments are spread over several weeks or months.

● Place your calendar(s) on a wall or bulletin board in your room where it is easily seen and accessible.

● Use a damp paper towel to clean your calendar off for the next month.

BREAK DOWN LONG-TERM ASSIGNMENTS

The process of breaking down long-term assignments into smaller units helps your left and right brain work together to organize specific steps that result in a completed project. Auditory, visual, and kinesthetic learners will benefit greatly by talking aloud while writing and reviewing the specific steps as needed. Help lower your stress level and raise your success level by following these steps (see *Sample: Monthly Calendar* on page 58).

1. Use the correct color of pen for each subject throughout this process.

2. Write in the date the assignment was given.
   Example: May 1, Science Report Assigned

3. Write in the date the assignment is due by using "Report Really Due." Then in the day before write, "Report Due" which is really Final Draft: Second Edit. Always give yourself one extra day to correct anything that may go wrong at the last minute. Plus, you can actually enjoy one extra day to relax and not panic. *Example:* May 30, Science Report Due (teacher's date is actually May 31)

4. Count the number of days between the assignment date and your "Report Due" date; divide that number into fourths, halves and three-fourths. Write "$^1/_4$", "$^1/_2$", and "$^3/_4$" on the appropriate dates.

5. Next, write three steps that should be completed for each date. For example:
   - On May 7: $^1/_4$ Sci. Rep.: topic narrowed, references checked out, double-check assignment
   - On May 15: $^1/_2$ Sci. Rep.: research completed, note cards organized, begin rough draft
   - On May 22: $^3/_4$ Sci. Rep.: first draft completed, edit final outline, begin works cited
   - Review dates for accuracy, conflicts, and assignments. Make adjustments as required. (For example, if you have a busy test schedule on May 15, move the $^1/_2$ to May 14 or May 16).

6. Work backwards from the "Report Due" date (May 30) to schedule 24 hours of not working on the assignment (see *"Hint for Written Assignments"* below). Schedule a "Final Draft: First Edit" and a "Final Draft: Second Edit."

7. Post a copy of the calendar in a place it will be seen every day as a reminder.

8. STICK TO YOUR SCHEDULE!

Hint: FOR WRITTEN ASSIGNMENTS

Always leave 24 hours between the time you finish your final edited draft and your final read-through before turning it in. This allows your brain to refocus on other things so upon r ereading the final draft you will catch mistakes that were not apparent on previous editing. See <u>Sample: Monthly Calendar</u> on page 58.

Hint: FOR READING ASSIGNMENTS

Break down the r eading by writing specific pages to be r ead each day (Mon. pp 1 –15, Tues. pp 16 –30, etc.) Remember to leave enough days to write your report, too. See <u>Sample: Monthly Calendar</u> on page 58.

MAY

SUNDAY	MONDAY	TUESDAY	WEDNESDAY	THURSDAY	FRIDAY	SATURDAY
	1 Sci. Report Assigned pp. 1–15	2 pp. 16–30	3 pp. 31–45	4 pp. 46–60	5	6
7 — topic narrowed — ref. checked — recheck assign.	8	9	10	11	12	13
14	15 — research complete — notes organized — begin rough draft	16	17	18	19	20
21	22 — 1st draft complete — edit final outline — works cited	23	24	25	26	27 Sci. Report FINAL DRAFT First Edit
28 Sci. Report (24 hours off)	29 Sci. Report FINAL DRAFT Second Edit	30 SCI. REPORT DUE	31 SCI. REPORT REALLY DUE			

$\mathcal{U}$SE A MONTHLY ASSIGNMENT CALENDAR IN YOUR BINDER

Why Keep a Monthly Calendar in Your Binder?

- Keeps you on track with each subject
- You can see an entire month at a time
- Serves as a reminder—even when your teacher forgets
- Stays with your binder so you can easily add to it during class
- Makes it easy to transfer assignments to your large home calendar

Keep Copies in Your Notebook

- Make several copies of page 60 and 3-hole punch each copy
- Place two to three copies in your ring binder behind each colored tab for each subject
- USE IT by continually writing in long-term assignments (anything due more than 24 hours from the current date)
- Check the binder assignment calendar briefly each night and transfer any new information to your home large calendar

Hint: *Always keep a calendar*

- *In a binder*
- *Inside your locker*
- *Inside your backpack*
- *On a bulletin board or wall in your room*

Monthly Assignment Calendar

Month _____

Class: _____

SUNDAY	MONDAY	TUESDAY	WEDNESDAY	THURSDAY	FRIDAY	SATURDAY

Guaranteed to successfully improve your study life!

What is Study Time?

It is a consistent, day-to-day, specific, scheduled time set aside to complete homework and review material which makes a habit of using effective study skills. It is important that you view this time as more than just a time to do homework. Even if nothing is due tomorrow, there is still "study time."

Why Use a Study Time?

- Using a specific study time develops a habit of studying.
- You will be more committed to studying if it becomes a daily habit.
- This single "habit" will successfully carry you through all your grade level challenges through college.
- It provides structured time to:
    - complete homework
    - keep current in all subject areas with review activities
    - make vocabulary/concept flash cards, mind maps, etc.
- It puts you in charge of your homework and study time, and stops constant parental reminders if you show the initiative to do it yourself.
- By using this time wisely, you will have more time for other things you want to do.

Setting and using your study time consistently—without being reminded by your parents—demonstrates your ability to effectively handle your own time. It is important that you view this habit as more than just a time to do homework. Getting parents "off your back" about homework and having the freedom to choose your own study time is really up to you.

The following sections on "Study Time" will teach you to:
- Schedule your own study time
- Follow rules for study time
- Apply appropriate study time activities

$\mathcal{S}$CHEDULING YOUR STUDY TIME ⎯⎯⎯⎯⎯⎯⎯⎯⎯⎯⎯⎯⎯

Use the "Sample: Daily Schedule" chart on page 64 to help find the best time to study

STEP 1 ☞ Compute the appropriate amount of time you need each day for your study block:

- Set study time by using the rule of 10 minutes per grade level, per day, five days a week
  Example: Grade 8 = 80 total minutes of study time each day

- Set study block time within the study time to make the best use of focused attention span/learning time per grade level by using this guideline:

  - Primary grades: 10–15 minute study block

  - Upper elementary: 20 minute study block

  - Middle/high school: 25–35 minute study block

  - College/adult: 45 minute study block

- Set break time to "recharge your brain" by using this guideline:

  - Primary grades: study 15/ break 10/ study 15 (Gr. 3 example)

  - Upper elementary: study 20/break 10/study 20/break 10/ study 10 (Gr. 5 example)

  - Middle/high school: study 30/break 10/study 30/break 10/ study 30 (Gr. 9 example)

STEP 2 ☞ Use one color of ink to write activities in the appropriate rectangles. Use horizontal or vertical lines to indicate repetitive activities that take up more than one block. Use one color to block out time for:

- Getting up

- School (include transportation/walking time to and from school)

- Eating dinner

- Going to bed

STEP 3 ☞ Use a second color to block out time for any regular, weekly commitments you have:

> *Examples:* music lessons, religious activities, sports, club meetings, family/friends activities

STEP 4 ☞ Use a third color to block out time for:

- Study time (remember to consider your best focused learning time when you are personally your most productive).

- Include your break time in addition to your appropriate study time.

- Use five rectangle blocks that touch by the corners or sides to avoid scattered study time (you cannot make studying a habit this way).

- Do not begin your study time later than 9:00 pm even if you are a "night person."

Hint: *Consider these successful hints.*

- Stick to your schedule for at least one week, then change it if necessary.

- Don't be afraid to change things around to be more productive.

- Be flexible and change something only if there is a good reason.

- Include some free time each day.

- Leave some time open for the unexpected.

- Become familiar with your schedule and make the schedule a habit.

- Post it and carry it with you so you can easily see it.

	SUN	MON	TUE	WED	THURS	FRI	SAT
5:00							
6:00		6:30 Get Up	Breakfast →→→→→→→				
7:00							
8:00		SCHOOL →→→→→→→→					
9:00							
10:00							
11:00							
12:00							
1:00							
2:00		↓	↓	↓	↓	↓	
3:00		Sports		Sports		Sports	
4:00		↓	Piano	↓		↓	
5:00							
6:00		Dinner →→→→→→→					
7:00	Study Time	→→→→→→→→					
8:00	↓	↓	↓	↓	↓		
9:00	9:30 Bedtime →→→						
10:00	↓	↓	↓	↓	↓		
11:00							
12:00	↓	↓	↓	↓	↓		

1. Study at your desk in your room without distractions.
   - Use the same place every time.
   - Set a purpose. Psychologically, your mind links the environment with the appropriate activity.
   - Use the study materials placed on, in, and near your desk for better use of your time.
   - Have materials at hand. You lose focus each time you have to go in search of needed material elsewhere in your house.

2. Create a comfortable environment (see *Elements for Better Learning* on page 28). Make sure your study area is:
   - Ventilated
   - Well-lit
   - Quiet (your room; not the kitchen/dining area, family/rec room, den, someone else's office)
   - Away from things that distract you
   - Well-equipped with reference materials and appropriate office supplies (see *Organize Your Materials!* on page 40)

3. Allow absolutely no distractions (see *Elements for Better Learning* on page 28) during your study time:
   - TV
   - music
   - food
   - windows in front of desk
   - disruptions by other family members/friends/phones
   - instant messaging or email
   - toys on desk top

4. Use your appropriately set study time (see *Scheduling Your Study Time* on page 62).

5. Use focused blocks within your study time (see *Scheduling Your Study Time* on page 62).

6. Use appropriate break times between study blocks (see *Scheduling Your Study Time* on page 62).
   - Leave your room to change your environment and give your brain a rest.
   - Do something physical (eat, walk, shoot baskets, play with pet, etc.).

7. For each "study block":
   - Begin by using the "Study Time Warmup" on page 70.
   - Write down short-term goals for that block
   - Use your estimated time (see *Use a Daily Assignment Sheet* on page 47) to know how much you can get done in a 30 minute block.
     Example: finish all math problems or read pp 47–52 in science and take notes
   - Set a timer for the appropriate study time, then place it out of sight.
   - Ask yourself periodically, "What am I trying to learn from this material?" and "What am I to know by the end of this study block?"
   - Make time to summarize aloud three concepts, facts, etc.
   - Ask yourself "How can I relate this to what I learned yesterday?"

8. Let everyone know when your study time is so they will not distract you.
   - Let someone else take phone messages during your study blocks so you can return the calls during your break time
   - Ask your parents to help with siblings so they are not a distraction
   - Post a sign on the outside of your closed bedroom door which says "STUDYING: PLEASE DO NOT DISTURB!"

9. Study every subject 10 minutes during your study time.
   - Helps you retain new information
   - Helps make learning more permanent
   - Gives you time to think through ideas and let information "soak in"
   - If you have homework in a subject, the 10 minutes are included in the time you do your homework. (It is not necessary to study an extra 10 minutes.)
   - If you do not have homework due tomorrow in a subject, follow the activities listed in *Appropriate Study Time Activities* on page 68.

10. Eliminate daydreaming to use quality, not quantity, study time.
   - Make a checkmark on a piece of scratch paper each time you catch yourself off focus (rest your hand on the paper and do not look when you make the mark).
   - Continually try to reduce the number of marks from one study block to the next.

11. Always study out loud to increase comprehension and memory.
   - Read text material aloud.
   - Talk aloud as you take notes after reading a paragraph.
   - Talk aloud while completing all homework assignments; this includes math problems, textbook reading assignments, etc. (except when reading for speed with a short story/novel, etc.).
   - Talk aloud when creating flash cards, study sheets, and graphic organizers.

12. Divide time and blocks among the subjects.
   - Study the hardest thing first, when your mind is fresh.
   - Leave routine and less difficult tasks for last.
       Example: recopying papers, organizing reports and files, creating tables of content for reports, etc.
   - Allow certain tasks to be spaced over several days:
       ▲ A little time on the task each night for five nights allows "reflective time"
       ▲ Material is better "soaked into the subconscious" when it is reviewed in a non-stressful situation
       ▲ This is much better for proofreading. You pick up many errors missed even the second time or third time of proofreading

13. Be sure you understand every assignment before you begin.

14. Take charge of your own study time.
   - Set the alarm on your watch to be at your desk at your set time
   - Keep all breaks to 10 minutes (no more, no less)
   - Do not depend on a reminder from anyone!

1. Complete school work due the next day and begin on all future assignments as time permits:

   ■ Complete assignments and immediately file in binder in appropriate place (see *Organize Your Materials!* on page 40).

   ■ Make lists of materials needed for class tomorrow, the next assignment, or an upcoming project.

   ■ Organize and plan long-term projects, papers, reports, etc. (see *Use a Monthly Calendar* on page 56).

   ■ Double-check calendar for conflicts, assignment due dates, etc.

2. Do any of the following activities for 10 minutes per subject per night (study time):

   ■ Review major concepts (see *Weekly Review (All Courses)* on page 74).

   ■ Make flash card for vocabulary/concepts (see *The Magic of Flash Cards* on page 112).

   ■ Review and memorize vocabulary words (see *Study Smart Vocabulary* on page 71 and *The Magic of Flash Cards* on page 112).

   ■ Review class or text notes.

   ■ Make study sheets (see *Constructing Study Sheets: Dump & Pile System* on page 117).

   ■ Make graphic organizers (see *Creating a Graphic Organizer* on page 119).

   ■ Make audio tapes of notes, important textbook sections, foreign language vocabulary (see *How to Study a Foreign Language* on page 195).

   ■ Reread textbook and notes.

   ■ Read ahead in textbook and take notes (see *Instructions for Super Note-Taking* on page 97 and *Text Note Taking* on page 101).

   ■ Reorganize, clean out, and update class notebooks.

   ■ Update calendars (see *Use a Monthly Calendar* on page 56, and *Use a Monthly Assignment Calendar in Your Binder* on page 59).

   ■ Make a "To Do" list (see *Take Control: Use a "To Do" List* on page 53).

   ■ Correct errors on past assignments, quizzes, texts, lab reports, etc.

   ■ Transfer completed assignments, notes, handouts, tests, lab reports from binders to home filing system folders (see *Organizing Your Materials!* on page 40).

3. Read ahead in:

- textbooks (see *Text Note Taking* on page 101 and *Instructions for Super Note Taking* on page 97)

- library books

- educational magazines (*Scientific American, Discover, National Geographic World,* etc.)

- test preparation workbooks for SAT/ACT tests if appropriate

4. Computer Work:

- Enter new data for each class.

- Write programs to help you with your homework.

- Work with appropriate educational software (prepare for SAT and/or ACT tests if appropriate).

- Do research or use online reference tools.

- Type up written assignments, make copies, etc.

5. To Check:

- Review "To Do" list and cross off completed tasks.

- Make a new "To Do" list for tomorrow (see *Take Control: Use a "To Do" List* on page 53).

- Check calendar: review target dates, add new assignment dates, break down and write in goals for long-term assignments, add meetings and activities (see *Use a Monthly Calendar* on page 56).

- Check your supply of materials in your home study area and your binders; make a list of the ones that need replenishing (see *Handy Supply Checklist* on page 44).

- Replenish new assignment sheet and monthly assignment calendars in your binder.

STUDY TIME WARMUP

Your mind operates much better when it is warmed up and ready to go. It is similar to starting up a car on a cold day. You have to put the key in the ignition, turn on the engine, and let the engine run for a little while to warm it up. Then, when you want to go somewhere, the whole car will run smoothly and efficiently!

Think of this analogy the next time you sit down to study. Here is a simple checklist to follow to help you focus your mind and warm it up so that you can make the very best use of your study time.

Warm up your mind every time you begin to study! Link the following questions and answers with physical actions:

PHYSICAL ACTION	QUESTION	ANSWER
1. Pull your chair out from your desk.	→ 1. What should I study first?	→ 1. Geometry
2. Sit down in your chair.	→ 2. What did we do in class today? What was the topic?	→ 2. Types of triangles
3. Open your book or notebook. Pick up your pencil.	→ 3. What are three specific concepts or new vocabulary words?	→ 3. Right triangle, obtuse triangle, acute triangle

Hint: When trying to form a habit with anything that must be done in a sequence, link the ideas with familiar sequential physical actions.

New terms can be a problem—especially if you don't understand them from the very beginning! But it doesn't have to be that way. In the long run, you can save much time, effort, and stress by developing an organized system to learn and review new vocabulary frequently. Use the *Study Smart Vocabulary Form* on page 72 and follow these easy steps. (Remember to talk aloud while you do this!)

1. As soon as a new vocabulary word is introduced in your textbook or lecture, immediately copy it into the *Vocabulary Word* column. Write the page number of the book or date of the class under the word for future reference.

2. Write your best guess of its definition in the *My Definition* column.

3. Look up the word in the dictionary and copy the pronunciation and dictionary definition into the correct columns.

4. Compare your definition to the dictionary definition. Reword your definition if necessary.

5. Make up an appropriate sentence using the word and write it in the *Sentence* column.

6. Write some related topics, subject areas, or synonyms in the *Related Concepts* column.

7. Make flash cards to help you memorize these important words. Follow the steps in *The Magic of Flash Cards* on page 112.

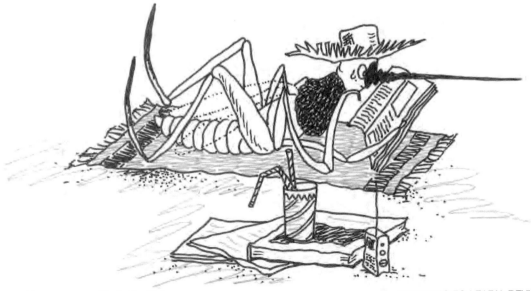

STUDY SMART VOCABULARY FORM

VOCABULARY WORD	PRONUNCIATION	MY DEFINITION	DICTIONARY DEFINITION	SENTENCE	RELATED CONCEPTS
1.					
2.					
3.					
4.					
5.					
6.					
7.					
8.					
9.					
10.					

Review! Review! Review! Sometimes it's easier said than done. But it can be made simpler and more organized to save you time, energy, and stress.

Consider the *Weekly Review (All Courses)* form on page 74 as a painless, organized method to keep you current with your studies. It's easy to follow these steps. (Remember to talk aloud while you do this!)

1. Try using the *Weekly Review* form for a week.

2. Use 5–10 minutes of the last study block in your study time of each week to complete this form. Be committed to continue it once you have started. Add to it daily.

3. Review this chart briefly each time you begin to study.

4. Be sure to include all information sources: textbook, class notes, handouts, etc.

WEEKLY REVIEW (ALL COURSES)

Name _____

Course _____

Dates: ___/___ to ___/___

COURSE TITLE	MAIN TOPICS COVERED	NEW VOCABULARY	WHAT I LEARNED	QUESTIONS I HAVE

	Assignment sheet is complete for each class/subject.
	Understand all assignments and due dates.
	Gather all necessary books, notebooks, materials, and supplies.
	Stop by the library/media center if necessary.
	Talk to or see any necessary persons.
	Review "To Do" list.

Post this checklist in your locker or on the inside cover of the binder you use for your last class of the day. This will help you avoid the "I forgot" syndrome!

CONCENTRATION is the ability to control your attention.

● distracting noises

● your body "condition" (too tired or hungry)

● boredom

● daydreaming

● worry

● dislike of subject

● wrong "time" of day

● TV, music, phone, food, studying on bed/floor

● overwhelming feeling about the task or assignment

● lack of commitment

● constant interruptions

● poor attention span

● indecision to study

● lack of sleep

● poor diet

- Intend to study and learn from the very beginning.

- Become interested in the subject so that your mind has a reason to read—to answer the questions.
    - Look for points of view.
    - Question and dare to disagree.
    - Predict the outcome.
    - See connections/relations within the information.

    - Know yourself.
        - Take advantage of your learning style and modality.
        - Use your positive aspects.
        - Know the time of day you study best.

        - Set clear and realistic goals.
            - Know what you are supposed to learn.
            - Concentrate on the focus of the material/information.
            - Briefly outline tasks to be completed within each study block.

            - Exclude distractions.
                - Keep a "distractions list" and continually try to reduce it. (We are often distracted by the same things again and again, but we usually are unaware of these things.)

                - Know why you are studying.
                  Ask yourself:
                    - Why do I need this knowledge or information?
                    - How is it relevant to me and what do I want to do with it?
                    - How will I apply this in the future?

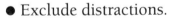

When You Finish an Assignment

REVIEW

- Briefly review as a summary activity.
- Skim/scan texts, notes, and handouts.
- Flip through 3" x 5" cards of vocabulary/concepts (see *The Magic of Flash Cards* on page 112).
- Talk to yourself.
- Recreate mind maps or other graphic organizers (see *Creating a Graphic Organizer* on page 119).
- In your mind, try to explain it to someone else.
- Reread the assignment and your homework to be sure you have completed what was expected.
- Talk about it with a friend/classmate/parent.
- Review again within 24 hours.

OVERLEARN

- Form a study group.
- Make up test questions about what you have learned.
- Keep a running list of new vocabulary words.
- Repeat the review steps.

EVALUATE

- Is your homework in the correct format, is it organized and easy to read?
- Is this your best effort?
- Did you learn what you intended to learn?
- Do you really know the information for which you will be held responsible?
- Is there a way you can improve?
- Can you restate, recite, or relate the material to show that you know it?

The *Study Prescription Worksheet* on page 80 is designed to be an activity which allows you to target and troubleshoot difficult classes, subjects, and materials and, more importantly, match each problem with a solution. Review this chapter for appropriate strategies, methods, hints, and approaches to basic skills to find and fix your "trouble" areas. Remember, for every problem there is a solution. It just may be that the process of finding the right solution is a bit frustrating at times. Be persistent and confident and don't forget to seek help if you need it.

STUDY PRESCRIPTION WORKSHEET

List Classes Here	List Problems with Studying for Each Class Here	List Solutions and Study Strategies for Each Class Here	Results	Rewards

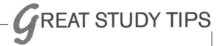

- Allow time for information to "soak in" and review every day. See *Rules for Study Time: The Backbone of Success* on page 65.

- Too many new ideas at one time are confusing, so break information down into small units/pieces. See *Constructing Study Sheets: Dump & Pile System* on page 117.

- The human brain can successfully process 6–7 ideas during one time period and maintain good retention of the information if enough repetition is used.

- It is less tiring to "spread out" study periods rather than to "cram." See *Scheduling Your Study Time* on page 62.

- Pace yourself by using calendars and "To Do" lists. See *Take Control: Use a "To Do" List* on page 53, *Use a Monthly Calendar* on page 56, and *Use a Monthly Assignment Calendar in your Binder* on page 59.

- Be organized. See *Organize Your Materials!* on page 40 and *The Wonders of Color Coding* on page 46.

- Complete the tasks/assignments that do not require great amounts of concentration alternately with more difficult tasks.

- Be sure your study activities are in tune with your intentions. See *Rules for Study Time: The Backbone of Success* on page 65.

- Begin with the most difficult tasks—and "get it done" so that it won't hang over your head!

- Make studying a habit. See *Scheduling Your Study Time* on page 62.

- Build on your learning strengths. See *The Magic of Flash Cards* on page 112, *Forming a Study Group* on page 215, *Mnemonics/Strategies for Improving Memory* on page 191, and *Be an Active Learner* on page 260.

- Seriously consider the effects of procrastination and how well you can do without them. See *Getting a Handle on Stress* on page 273.

- Examine your priorities and how you can adjust your behavior to make your life easier and more successful. See *Problem Solving* on page 264, and *Improve Your Thinking Skills* on page 262.

- Become aware of your time management patterns and change them gradually to better meet your needs. See *Scheduling Your Study Time* on page 62.

- Learn to use spare moments (standing in line, waiting for someone or something, etc.). See *The Magic of Flash Cards* on page 112.

- Make sure you understand the assignment before leaving class. Use your assignment sheet. See *Use a Daily Assignment Sheet* on page 47.

- Set reasonable time limits for yourself. See *Use a Daily Assignment Sheet* on page 47, and *Take Control: Use a "To Do" List* on page 53.

- Give yourself enough time to do a good job and always predict the amount of time and effort required to complete the task. Go for quality! See *Use a Daily Assignment Sheet* on page 47, and *Take Control: Use a "To Do" List* on page 53.

- Don't spread yourself too thin. Consider your commitments and the priority of each. See *Take Control: Use a "To Do" List* on page 53 , and *Getting a Handle on Stress* on page 273.

- Really enjoy your "free time."

- Have a positive attitude about learning.

- Be willing to accept improvement suggestions and act on them.

- It's OK to dislike the assignment or task, but do it anyway!

- Good grades most often are lost due to a lack of organization rather than a lack of information.

- Concentration is the biggest problem when studying, so get rid of distractions and use focusing techniques.

- Review the information just before you go to bed by using flash cards and graphic organizers. See *The Magic of Flash Cards* on page 112, *Elements for Better Learning* on page 28, and *What Slows You Down & How to Improve* on page 168.

- Prop reading material at a 45-degree angle so that your eyes will be less tired.

- Seek help if you don't understand something or if you are having problems.

- Get to know someone in every class you have. You can borrow or trade books, study together, and ask each other questions about assignments.

- Comprehend what you learn—don't just memorize! See *Important Comprehension Skills* on page 166, and *Thinking . . . Odds and Ends* on page 269.

STUDY

⬇

LEARN

⬇

REVIEW

⬇

OVERLEARN

⬇

EVALUATE

⬇

HIGHER TEST SCORES AND GRADES

⬇

MORE SELF-CONFIDENCE

⬇

...THE EASIER LEARNING BECOMES!

NOTE-TAKING SKILLS

FOCUS ON
NOTE-TAKING SKILLS

1. Use intentional, focused listening with a positive attitude.

2. Be an active listener and note taker.

3. Listen 80% and write 20% of the time.

4. Continually add to your personal shorthand system.

5. Review your notes regularly.

6. Match your subject to the right note-taking format.

7. Edit your notes frequently into graphic organizer study sheets.

8. Use color, shapes, and placement to your learning advantage.

9. Keep notes together in an organized binder.

10. Tune out distractions.

11. Remember the results of your learning styles assessment. Choose note-taking tools that focus on your strengths and minimize your weaknesses.

OVERVIEW OF NOTE-TAKING SKILLS

Note Taking
Lecture
Text
Problems/ Solutions
Tips
Teacher Inventory
Activities
Examples
Problems/ Solutions
Tips
Examples
Editing
Study Sheets

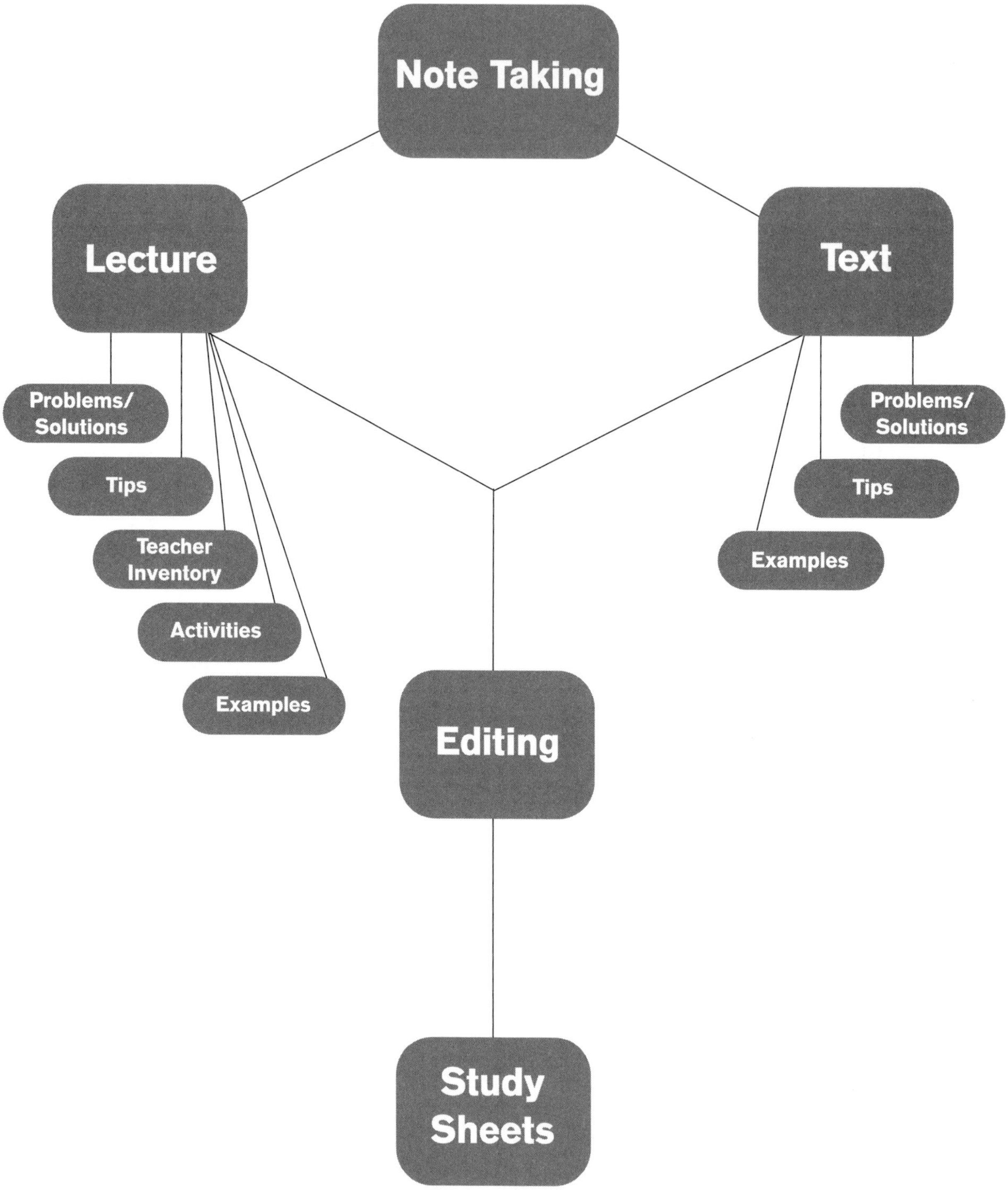

Learning and Great Grades!

Listening and note taking are two critical classroom survival skills. Without intentional, focused listening, taking accurate notes is impossible. Without effective class notes, learning and retention are reduced greatly.

To be a successful student, good study tools must be correctly and consistently applied with ease. By first evaluating current skills and then integrating new techniques, note taking can become the tool that ensures success, makes studying for tests easier, and shortens study time.

Note taking should be one of your top priorities among all of the study skills. It provides a reference that may be reviewed many times as an aid to memory. Good note-taking methods will help the ongoing process of learning become more meaningful. Learn to become highly efficient and effective by combining text reading notes with class lecture notes and creating study sheets to reduce time and stress. Follow the strategies in this chapter to make your life easier.

Taking excellent textbook and lecture notes is not impossible if you have an organized system. This chapter will provide solutions to common note-taking problems:

- Reading texts for comprehension/understanding
- Rereading pages of text
- Identifying main ideas and details in lecture
- Writing faster to keep up with lecturer
- Editing notes
- Organizing text and class notes for tests

As you review these note-taking techniques, focus on the elements that best fit your learning modality: visual, auditory, or kinesthetic.

A few suggested note-taking aids for the three modalities are:

VISUAL:	AUDITORY:	KINESTHETIC:
• Watch for important vocabulary words • Chunk information together on a page • Use drawings, charts, and graphs	• Say vocabulary words out loud • Listen carefully from the very beginning • Read and repeat things orally	• Use graphic organizers • Associate feelings with concept/information • Flip through vocabulary cards often

Set Your Intentions
for Reading and Lecture Note Taking

Be Prepared to Take Good Notes

Use Super Note-Taking System

Identify and Improve Note-Taking Problems

Construct Study Sheets

Make Flash Cards

Create Graphic Organizers

LEARN! REMEMBER!
GET GREAT GRADES!

INPUT OVERLOAD

- One third of our "awake time" is spent listening.
- Attention wanders at times.

BRAIN POWER

- The brain is capable of understanding speech at 600 words per minute.
- The average person speaks 100 to 140 words per minute.
- What does your mind do with all of the "leftover" time?

PHYSICAL NOISE

- Sounds in the environment interfere.
- Physical surroundings are uncomfortable.
- Fatigue distracts.

PERSONAL CONCERNS

- Emotional problems and/or thoughts occupy the mind and block out auditory input.

TALKING SEEMS MORE IMPORTANT

LISTENING SKILLS NOT TAUGHT

- Listening skills not continually/consistently practiced.

"TUNE IN" TOO LATE

- Individuals do not listen from the start of the lecture/conversation.

NOT LISTENING AHEAD

- Individuals do not process and remember/associate what is being said now with the goal of applying the information that will be given in the future.

- "Set" your mind—intend to listen.

- Listen to what is being said—don't allow your mind to wander.

- Clarify why you are listening—set a purpose and goal.

- Clarify continually (to yourself) what is being said.

- Keep your mind active—take notes.

- Resist distractions (physical, emotional, mental).

- Involve yourself—think of examples as the speaker talks.

- Listen very closely to introductory and concluding remarks/ideas.

- Anticipate what is coming next (this is the most difficult yet the most effective for your memory). Keep an open mind.

- Pay attention to "speaker cues" (voice, physical motions, rate of speech) for main ideas.

- Think of questions while listening (helps to organize thoughts).

- Identify speaker's method of organization for delivering the information.

- Constantly try to link concepts and main ideas with details as well as cause/effect and problem-solving techniques.

- Listen for what is *not said* as well as what is *said*.

- Identify facts and opinions.

- Listen to class discussions carefully and make note of any points the speaker reinforces or repeats.

- Always summarize the information and immediately write three or more main ideas.

Each individual should develop a "Personal Shorthand System" to become more efficient and effective in note-taking skills. This will allow you to put more information on paper with less effort and stress in less time.

This system should be personalized by the individual in order to fully gain the most benefit from the process and product. This also allows for a more consistent and natural system for years to come.

STEP 1 ☞ Look over your notes from recent classes to see how many times you repeat the same words. Make a list of these "generic" words. These words should be ones you use in many of your classes.

STEP 2 ☞ Decide upon a symbol or abbreviation for each word so that you can write these words faster. Make a list on a 3" x 5" card of the words and their abbreviations/symbols.

STEP 3 ☞ Place the 3" x 5" card on your desk at school whenever you need to take notes. Use it as a reference to practice using the symbols/abbreviations in place of the words you normally write out.

STEP 4 ☞ Add to your list whenever you find yourself rewriting the same words throughout the day.

STEP 5 ☞ Use this same card for two consecutive weeks to make your new "Personal Shorthand System" an easy and successful habit.

Here are a few examples to get you started:

b/c = because	w/o = without
∴ = therefore	gov = government
w/ = with	b/f = before
➡ = to follow	rt = right
cont. = continue	* = important
+, & = and	intro = introduction

STEP 6   ☞ When you are taking notes from a "specialized lecture" in which a specific topic will be covered (requiring a special, repeated vocabulary), you will need to create a code just for this one-time purpose. Be sure to listen carefully, especially at the beginning of class when the teacher might introduce new vocabulary to be used during that lecture.

        ☞ Also, be alert and watch for written words and phrases on the overhead, dry-erase/chalk board throughout the class period. Add these to your list. Later, during study time, fill in the entire words if you need to do so.

        ☞ You'll always know what you abbreviated because your "key" will be on the paper. It can also serve as a study guide to point out important vocabulary words. Make a box in the upper left corner of a piece of paper and write the symbols and their meanings for this specific purpose in the box. Be sure to leave space for additions as you may need to add some as the lecture progresses. You always can refer to this box during the lecture and when you review/edit your notes.

RC = rock cycle
 S = sedimentary
 M = metamorphic
 I = igneous

Earth Science
Rachelle Blair
Mar. 20

Class Notes: Rock Cycle

Memory and comprehension greatly improve when you listen 80% of the time and write 20% of the time.

You remember more topics, sub-topics, details, and examples when you group information together when you read and take notes.

Your mind remembers horizontal and vertical space on a paper as well as what is written on it.

Taking notes from one margin to the other across the page is the least effective way to remember what you just wrote.

Why Use This System?

The basic structure of this Cornell note-taking system has be used for many years. It is modified here to include more details so that you will know specifically how and why to take good notes and make life much easier for yourself! This super note-taking method is a great way to:

● reduce major stress when taking class notes by taking previously written text notes back into class as a listening guide

● simply underline repeated information the teacher says in the text column

● increase your memory by listening more and writing less

● combine text and class notes with important vocabulary words

● group information around words listed in a separate column

● save time by writing brief and concise notes in the margins

● distinguish the source of information quickly (text or class notes or both)

Refer often to *Sample: Note-Taking Form* on page 99 for a better understanding of the following steps.

YOU CAN LEARN TO TAKE NOTES
THE EASY WAY!

This note-taking method is a super way to combine text and class notes with important vocabulary words. It will allow you to keep important information together according to major concepts and save you time and stress in class. Simply use this form for taking text notes and then take the same paper into class.

Refer to *Sample: Note-Taking Form* on page 99 while reading through these steps. It's easier than you think!

"KEY WORD" COLUMN

- Write in key words (bold, italicized, underlined, or colored new vocabulary words).

- Write the page number immediately below the word for quick reference.

- Use these words as the center shape in graphic organizers (see *Graphic Organizers* on pages 124–132).

- Use these words for your "Fantastic Flash Cards" (see *The Magic of Flash Cards* on page 112).

"TEXT NOTES" COLUMN

- Take notes from the reading assignment.

- Notice organizational pattern: main topic, sub-topics, examples/details, sub-examples/details.

- Use spaces and indentations (helps group information for your memory).

- Use bullets to differentiate main topics, sub-topics, details/examples, sub-details

- Do not use formal lettering or numbering systems (I, II, III, A, 1, 2, 3, a, b, c, etc.) because:
  - ▲ They are distracting.
  - ▲ They focus on the format of your notes rather than on the information.

- Do not use complete sentences/long phrases.
  - ▲ Use only three to four words together.
  - ▲ The simpler you keep it, the better you will remember it.

- Leave spaces between concepts to allow for later additions.

"CLASS NOTES" COLUMN

- Take this same paper to class for the lecture.

- Listen carefully to lectures as well as class discussions, student comments, etc.

- Use this paper as your listening guide.

- Use words in "Key Word" column as a guide to locate material quickly.
  - ▲ If the teacher presents information in a different order than your textbook notes, use these words to find the topic.

- Whenever lecture information is the same as notes in the "Text Notes" column, simply underline it. You won't have to rewrite it this time, just listen.

- Remember, writing less and listening more while you take notes helps you to really learn the information and remember it much longer.

- Whenever new information is given in class lecture but not found in the "Text Column", you should write it in the "Class Notes" column.

USE THESE NOTES

- To quiz yourself each study time
  - ▲ Place a blank paper over the "text notes" and "class notes" columns.
  - ▲ Orally repeat all information you can remember about the first key word.
  - ▲ Slide the blank paper down to reveal all information in the two columns regarding that concept.
  - ▲ Reread both columns and check yourself for accuracy.
  - ▲ Repeat aloud any information you missed.

- To create graphic organizers
  (See *Creating a Graphic Organizer* on page 119.)
  - ▲ Use words in the "Key Word" column as the center shape.

- To create fantastic flash cards
  (See *The Magic of Flash Cards* on page 112.)

Vocabulary Abbreviation Key

    C—Cetacea

    BW—baleen whales

    H—humpbacks

Class	*Science*
Date	*9/27*
Name	*Rachelle Blair*
	Oceanography Unit

Key Word	Text Notes	Class Notes
Cetacea 44	*Cetacea (whales)*	

baleen 45	*Baleen whales (main topic)*
	• *use baleens: (sub topic)*
	  no teeth (detail)
	    • *feather-like*
	    • *strain plankton*
	• *size:*
	    • *20'–100'*
	• *travel in pods*
	    • *5–30 whales*
	    • *male leader*
	• *three types:*
	    • *humpback (example)*
	    • *blue*
	    • *fin*
		• *pleated throat*
		    • *gulp in water*
		    • *push back thru baleen*
		      • *capture plankton*
		• *hunted for:*
		    • *meat*
		    • *oil (blubber)*
		    • *bone*

humpback 46	*humpbacks*
	• *known for: songs/males*
	• *size:*
	    • *62'*
	    • *53 tons*
		• *coloration: (sub topic)*
		    • *black (detail)*
		      • *except parts/*
		        underside
		        (sub detail)

NOTE-TAKING FORM

Vocabulary Abbreviation Key

Class _____

Date _____

Name _____

_____

Key Word	Text Notes	Class Notes

Why Take Notes?

Writing down notes as an aid to jog your memory to recall what you read is always a great idea. To help you save time and effort in the long run, you may have to change your thinking about when you usually read text material—from normally after a lecture on the same topic or just before a test, to just before you go to class for the lecture.

Begin to think of the lecture part of class time as review of concepts you have already learned in your mind. When your teacher assigns reading in preparation for the next class, it is to your advantage to follow through and read the material as suggested, because this:

- Enables you to take notes in a more relaxed atmosphere during your study time at home a day or so before you sit through the lecture in class. You will have all the time you need to take good, effective notes.

- Provides the time you need to understand and learn new information, not just jot down notes in class only to really "learn them later."

- Provides you with an excellent "listening guide" when you take these notes into class (see *Super Note-Taking System* on page 96).

- Gives you time to become acquainted with new vocabulary words; their definitions and how they are used; new concepts and details; and an overview of new material and how it all "fits together."

All too often, students do not read and take text notes ahead, only to find taking class notes from lectures very frustrating. They try to simultaneously write down what is presented in class and hear it for the first time. Most students who function this way often find themselves leaving class in a daze and muttering that they didn't understand anything and they will "learn it later" when they review their notes. This approach works against comprehension and memory skills, causes undue stress, increases study time, and leads to a feeling of frustration rather than competence. In short, it's doing it the hard way.

Carefully follow the steps in the *Super Note-Taking System* section on page 96 and learn how to take notes the easy way and combine text and class notes for great success and increased learning. You won't believe just how easy it can be!

*T*EXT NOTE TAKING

Before You Begin . . .

STEP 1 ☞ Review the steps of pre-reading the chapter or unit (see *SQ3R* on page 162 to help you focus on your reading assignment).

STEP 2 ☞ Set yourself up for memory and comprehension success by giving your mind a purpose to read. If it has a specific purpose to retain information before you actually begin reading, you probably will not have to reread it—and that saves time!

STEP 3 ☞ Read just one paragraph at a time (without taking notes) for these three categories:
- Main topic
- Sub-topic
- Details and Examples

STEP 4 ☞ Begin taking notes using the steps given in the *Super Note-Taking System* on page 96.

 ©Incentive Publications, Inc., Nashville, TN

*I*DENTIFY TEXT NOTE-TAKING PROBLEMS
THEN FIND SOLUTIONS HERE:

PROBLEMS ➡	SOLUTIONS
When is the best time to read the textbook?	• *Text Note Taking* on page 101 • *Study Time* on page 61
I can't tell what's important when taking text notes.	• *Text Note Taking* on page 101 • *Reading Skills* on page 145
I have trouble grouping all the details around a main topic.	• *Note-Taking Form* on page 100
I don't know how much to write when taking text notes.	• *Instructions for Super Note-Taking System, Text Notes Column* on page 97 • *How to Edit and Review Notes* on page 116
I have trouble staying focused and have to reread the text often.	• *Rules for Study Time* on page 65 • *Text Note Taking* Steps 2–3 on page 102 • *Reading* on page 146 • *Great Study Tips* on page 82
I have trouble understanding and remembering what I read.	• *Text Note Taking* Steps 2–3 on page 102 • *Reading* on page 146 • *Memory* on page 183 • *Good Study/Review Questions* on page 271 • *What Anyone Needs to Do to Think* on page 272 • *In Order to Learn Anything* on page 272
I don't understand how all the information fits together.	• *Sample: Note-Taking Form* on page 99 • *Creating a Graphic Organizer* on page 119 • *Reading* on page 146 • *Good Study/Review Questions* on page 271 • *Plan of Attack for Independent Study* on page 285
I'm overwhelmed by the number of pages I need to study for a test!	• *Constructing Study Sheets: Dump & Pile System* on page 114

In Reading/Text:

PROBLEMS ➡	SOLUTIONS
The text is boring.	Break the information into small units. Set a goal of completing so many units, then reward yourself. See *SQ3R* on page 162 to give your mind a reference and purpose to read.
Your mind wanders.	Reading one paragraph at a time, make a check mark on a separate sheet of paper each time you realize that your mind is wandering. Set a goal of making fewer check marks for each assignment.
The vocabulary is difficult.	Using one paragraph, try to read through the information without stopping. Use context clues as much as possible. After reading, look up difficult words and write the definitions.
There's too much material and not enough time.	Form a study group. Divide the material to be covered and assign specific pages, chapters, etc., to each member. Ask each member to take thorough notes and study the information. Return to the group and orally share the assigned material. Give photocopies of all notes to every group member. (However, there is no substitute for reading it yourself in addition to forming a study group.)
You still don't understand the material after reading it numerous times.	Form a study group (see above) and talk it through with friends. Seek tutors in your school or community. Ask your teacher for help.

- Within two weeks you forget 80% of what you hear!
- Within four weeks you remember only 5% of what you heard!
- You are 10 times more likely to remember information if you write it down!

Why Take Notes?

Because our memories fade quickly and teachers expect us to remember and apply facts we learn, it is essential to write information so that it can be used at a later time. Learning to take effective and efficient notes helps you to be an active learner and involves you in the process of learning. Organized note taking from lectures will lead to longer memory and better grades!

BEFORE CLASS

- At home, during your study time the day before each class, use the 10-minutes-per-subject rule. (See *Rules for Study Time: The Backbone of Success* on page 65):
  - Skim or review any text/material assigned or notes from previous classes.
  - Organize all needed materials for binders and backpacks at home.
    - ▲ Notebook paper, assignment sheets
    - ▲ Pens, highlighters, pencils
    - ▲ Necessary handouts, past assignments, assignments in progress

- At school:
  - Check that you have the appropriate text, binder, and needed materials from your locker or backpack.
  - Plan to arrive in class with enough time to get organized.
  - Save time between classes by gathering materials for two or three consecutive classes so you won't have to go back to your locker between every class.

- In the classroom:
  - Sit in the front of the room.
    - ▲ Helps avoid distractions from those sitting in front of you
    - ▲ Sitting in the teacher's line of vision helps you to stay focused and "in tune."
  - Open your text to the proper place.

- Organize appropriate homework assignments, handouts, lab reports, etc. for easy access during class.
- Place your Personal Shorthand System 3" x 5" card on the desk top (see *Personal Shorthand System* on page 93).
- Use your note-taking form (see *Note-Taking Form* on page 100) to add lecture notes to text notes.
- If taking new notes for class, date and title your note-taking paper ahead of time to be prepared for focused listening at the beginning of class.
- Set your mind to listen and write from the very beginning of class:
  - ▲ Listening 80% of the time and writing 20% greatly increases comprehension and memory.
  - ▲ Intend to be an active listener and note taker.

DURING CLASS

- Listen and write any teacher instructions or rules for note taking or specific required materials.

- Write the topic for that class period under the heading on your paper.

- Listen for and write down key vocabulary words:
  - The first few minutes of class most teachers say, write, or point to key vocabulary words to be included in that lecture.
  - Write these down immediately in the "Key Vocabulary" box on your paper and create appropriate abbreviations (See *Note-Taking Form* on page 100 and *Personal Shorthand System* on page 93).

- Use your Personal Shorthand System throughout the class (see *Personal Shorthand System* on page 93).

- Pay close attention to introduction information (first few minutes) and summary information (last few minutes) because both usually contain the main ideas the teacher wants to convey.

- Stay focused.

- To help your mind stay focused, constantly ask yourself questions about the material being presented:
  - What do I already know about this?
  - Where did I hear/read about this topic before?

- What comes next?
- What does this have to do with yesterday's class?
- Where is he/she going with this information?
- How does this link with the text/handout material?

● Use your assignment sheet every class period:
  - Place it in an "easy to access" part of your binder.
  - Write assignments/test dates in the same place all the time.

● Watch for signals that indicate important information.

● Copy whatever the teacher writes on the board or overhead.

● Underline or highlight whatever the teacher discusses from a handout.

● Always write definitions and listings:
  - "The four steps in this process . . ."
  - "Seven characteristics are . . ."
  - "The two causes are . . ."
  - "These four reasons are . . ."

● Listen for important remarks such as:
  - "And don't forget . . ."
  - "This is an important reason . . ."
  - "Pay special/close attention to . . ."
  - "The basic idea is . . ."
  - ". . . and I'll keep coming back to the idea that . . ."

● Note the teacher's physical gestures. Every speaker demonstrates specific "body language" that signals important information:
  - Pointing
  - Listing with fingers
  - Facial expressions
  - Stepping forward
  - Pounding on the desk
  - Folding/unfolding arms
  - Raising arms or hands
  - Standing, then sitting; sitting, then standing

- Pacing, stopping, then turning to face the class
- Walking up and down desk aisles then stopping or turning
- Raised hands/fingers from behind a podium
- Shifting body position to show a hip, leg, etc. from behind a podium

- Listen to the teacher's change in voice to signal important information:
  - Change in speed
  - Change in volume
  - Change in pitch

- Always note repeated information
  - Make hash marks, stars, or other symbols in left column. Use "Key Word" column (see *Note-Taking Form* on page 100).
  - Don't hesitate to raise your hand and ask a question—one third of the class is thinking about the same question
  - Teachers like students who show interest and curiosity because it demonstrates you are paying attention and focused on the information.

- Don't stop taking notes when the teacher isn't talking:
  - Take notes from class discussions and presentations, student comments, diagrams and charts shown in class, overhead transparencies, etc.

- Circle any unclear information and seek an answer from your teacher.

AFTER CLASS

- Ask the teacher any questions when appropriate.

- Ask another student to help you fill in any notes you didn't get during class.

- Summarize your notes. Use a graphic organizer (see *Creating a Graphic Organizer* on page 119).

- Review and edit your notes within 24 hours.

- Make new vocabulary flash cards on every subject daily (see *The Magic of Flash Cards* on page 112).

PROBLEMS ➡	SOLUTIONS
I have trouble staying focused when listening to the teacher.	• *Rules for Study Time, Rule 10* on page 67 • *Why We Don't Listen* on page 91 • *Listening Skills* on page 92 • *Lecture Note Taking* on page 105
I can't tell what's important when taking class notes.	• *Lecture Note Taking* on page 105
I can't write fast enough during lectures.	• *Personal Shorthand System* on page 93 • *Super Note-Taking System* on page 96 • *Sample: Note-Taking Form* on page 99
I have trouble organizing my notes while I take notes.	• *Super Note-Taking System* on page 96 • *Sample: Note-Taking Form* on page 99
I have trouble combining class and text notes.	• *Super Note-Taking System* on page 96 • *Instructions for Super Note Taking* on page 97 • *Sample: Note-Taking Form* on page 99 • *Constructing Study Sheets* on page 117 • *Creating A Graphic Organizer* on page 119
I don't know what to do with my notes once I have them.	• *Constructing Study Sheets* on page 117 • *Creating A Graphic Organizer* on page 119

HINTS FOR BETTER LECTURE NOTE TAKING

SPEAKER ➡	NOTES
1. The speaker is well-organized.	1. Notes are easy to take and will be well-organized.
2. The speaker talks too fast, speaks in a monotone, or has a speech problem.	2. Try to adjust your ears and mind quickly; be a good listener.
3. The speaker is boring.	3. Force yourself to become an "active listener." Guess what's coming next, make connecting points with the material presented, and think of questions to ask. Using a piece of scratch paper, rest your hand on it when not taking notes. Without looking down, make a check mark on the paper when your mind starts to wander. This physical action will help your mind to refocus. Try for fewer marks each day.
4. The speaker uses difficult or unknown vocabulary.	4. Read the text the speaker will cover before the lecture. Wait until after the lecture to look up difficult words.
5. The speaker leafs through the text while speaking.	5. Be sure to have your text close at hand. Identify or note important paragraphs.
6. The speaker rambles.	6. Write something about each topic mentioned. Listen for introductory and concluding statements.
7. The speaker digresses to relate personal experiences and examples.	7. Rest your mind, but be alert to any important main ideas or details.
8. You do not like the speaker.	8. Don't waste time or energy thinking about why you do not like the speaker. You need the information, give yourself permission not to like the speaker, then get on with note taking!

TEACHER INVENTORY

Teacher's Name	Hints, Systems, Methods Verbal/Non-Verbal Clues	Materials Most Often Used	I Will Use

Why Make Flash Cards?

Flash cards are the most successful learning tool for memorizing new vocabulary, concepts with definitions, etc. Index cards are inexpensive, easy to organize and carry in a pocket or backpack, simple to store, and friendly to use. They require very little time to make and pay big dividends when you need to recall information for a test, speech, or presentation. In short, making and using them is very hard to beat! They work with how your brain learns because they:

● Target important vocabulary words and concepts

● Use construction and review steps in patterns of three (a magic number for your brain power) to learn and memorize information

● Encourage active learning (physically manipulating materials to learn), not passive learning (rereading your notes over and over)

● Reduce frustration and stress for tests

● Promote long term memory with frequent and consistent review

● Provide easy and organized access to vocabulary for the entire semester or year

MATERIALS YOU WILL NEED:

■ list of vocabulary words, words in "key word" column in text/lecture notes (See *Sample: Note-Taking Form* on page 99)

  ▲ break your list into sets of three words and their definitions by drawing appropriate lines

  ▲ if it is distracting to you to see the entire list at once, fan-fold your paper on the lines so you can concentrate on only three words at a time

■ 3" x 5" index cards

  ▲ use bright or pastel cards (color coordinate with subject areas—see *The Wonders of Color Coding* on page 46)

■ blue/black ink pen

■ hand-held paper punch

■ 1-inch split rings

■ various colored individual tabs

■ 3" x 5" card plastic storage box

■ rubber bands

■ small Post-it® Notes

Steps to Making Flash Cards

STEP 1 ☞ Say the word out loud

STEP 2 ☞ Spell the word out loud as you watch yourself write it down in the middle of one side of the card

STEP 3 ☞ Say the word again as you look at the whole word

STEP 4 ☞ Turn the card over by flipping the bottom of the card to the top (not side to side; this will allow you to read both sides when flipping them using the split ring in Step 14)

STEP 5 ☞ Say the definition out loud

STEP 6 ☞ Write the definition and say each word out loud (it's usually not important to spell each word in the definition) as you see yourself write it

STEP 7 ☞ Say aloud the word that is on the front. You may want to get out of your chair and become more active by pacing around your room while you follow Steps 7–11

STEP 8 ☞ Turn the card over and check to see if you were correct

STEP 9 ☞ Say the definition

STEP 10 ☞ Turn the card over and check to see if you were correct

STEP 11 ☞ Repeat steps 7–8

STEP 12 ☞ Repeat steps 1–11 for the next two words

STEP 13 ☞ Punch holes in the upper right or left corner of each card

STEP 14 ☞ Place the set of three 3" x 5" cards on a split ring

STEP 15 ☞ Quiz yourself

- Read aloud the word on the front of the first card and say aloud the matching answer
- Flip the card over to check your answer
- Repeat through all remaining cards

- Turn the set of three over and quiz yourself the same way except saying the definitions first and the words second
- Turn over one more time and say the words first and the definitions, each time flipping the cards to check on your answers. Remember to talk out loud!

STEP 16 ☞ Add sets of three cards, one at a time, until you have completed your list of new terms
  - Repeat all of the steps with each new card

Now Memorize Your Flash Cards

You must actively review the cards two to three times a week.

● Flip through all of the cards, one by one, by saying the words first and the definitions second, flipping each card over to check your answer

● Then flip through them again, one by one, saying the definition first and the word second, flipping each card over to check your answer.

● The best time to memorize and review is immediately before going to sleep at night.

● Your subconscious "replays" the last thing you "loaded in" while you were conscious.

● Review for 10 minutes then go to sleep

STUDY WHILE YOU SHOWER!
Pressed for time? This is a great trick!

● Place a 3″ x 5″ card in a sealable plastic bag.

● Using a small piece of duct tape, adhere the bag to the shower wall at eye level so the bottom of the bag is at the top and the zip portion is at the bottom (this will keep water from collecting in the bag). You should be able to read the back of the card when flipped up.

● Repeat these steps using all your flash cards, a box of bags, and a roll of duct tape until you have a row or two around all the walls.

● Simply replace the flash cards whenever appropriate.

Hint: • *Always "load" information into your mind in both directions (word-to-definition and definition-to-word). The order in which you memorize material is the same order in which you will recall it. By consistently alternating the words and definitions you will be able to retrieve either one easily, which saves time and frustration — especially on matching sections of tests.*

• *Keep current! Make new cards each night in each subject. It is far less stressful to make a few at a time than fifty the night before a test.*

• *Review the cards once each week, even after a test on that topic. This makes midterm and final exams easier and more successful.*

Storing Your Flash Cards

After completing a unit/test, store your flash cards for future use (midterm and semester/final exams):

● Use a color-coordinated tab for each subject—red for math, green for science, etc.(See *The Wonders of Color Coding* on page 46).
● Label each with generic titles to reuse year after year ("Math" instead of "Algebra").
● Place tabs in alternating spaces on the tops of color-coordinated 3″ x 5″ cards.
● Place these 3″ x 5″ card subject dividers in the plastic storage box.
● Remove all cards from split rings.
● Rubber band them together.
● Label them with a Post-it® Note (main topic, unit/chapters, specific text pages, etc.).
● Place them behind the appropriate, tabbed subject.
● You can easily find them to review at any time!

HOW TO EDIT AND REVIEW NOTES

WHAT IS IT?
- A system of correcting, revising, and adding to your text or lecture notes

WHY EDIT?
- To make your notes more accurate, complete, easier to understand, and easier to remember
- To organize your notes

HOW TO EDIT:
- Read your notes.
- Plan to spend 5 to 10 minutes per one set of notes.
- Try to edit within 24 hours after taking the notes.
- Turn headings into questions and try to answer them.
- Replace the shorthand system with complete thoughts where needed.
- Clarify points and meanings and make connections.
- Add personal insights.
- List questions to ask the teacher.
- Use a recall clue system:
  - ▲ Leave a 1"– 2" left margin.
  - ▲ When editing notes, add words to trigger your memory.
  - ▲ Cover the right side of the paper and use the words in the column to test yourself as you edit.

Why Make Study Sheets?

Study sheets are summary notes that you can use to:

● combine lecture and text notes as well as research information and your own ideas

● force you to concentrate on your notes while you rewrite the main ideas and important details one more time

● become an active learner and more clearly see relationships between main concepts and details.

● reduce your number of notes from a large number into an efficient and effective format with fewer pages to study

● keep track of changing or additional information

● reduce the amount of study time spent when a test is near—study sheets actually make studying easier as you progress through the process

STEP 1 ☞ Gather all your class/text notes, handouts, etc., for one subject.

STEP 2 ☞ Spread all your notes, etc. on a countertop, floor or other flat surface where you can easily see them. (This is the DUMP part!)
- Remember to take notes on only one side of the paper so you are able to see all the information without flipping papers.

STEP 3 ☞ Decide on the best way to organize the material.
- Spend a few minutes and brainstorm major topics of the chapter, unit, etc.
- Write each topic on a separate 3" x 5" card.
- Place the cards in a row in an empty space on the countertop, floor, etc.
- Be sure to place them in order if that is important (chronological, by date of class lecture, sequential, etc.).

STEP 4 ☞ Scan all notes.
- Keep in mind your major topics written on the 3" x 5" cards.
- Collect all pages that pertain to the first 3" x 5" card topic.
- Cut the page apart if one or more topics are on the same page.

CONSTRUCTING STUDY SHEETS: (continued)
DUMP & PILE SYSTEM

STEP 5 ☞ Stack each pile (This is the PILE part!)

- Lay the pages of notes under the first 3" x 5" topic card.
- Continue to gather remainder of notes in the same manner.
- Pile these notes under the appropriate topic cards.
- All notes should now be broken down in respective piles and labeled with the card on top.

STEP 6 ☞ Color code.

- Beginning with the first stack of papers under one major topic, use highlighters (yellow, pink, green, blue) to identify major concepts and supporting details.
- Use a different color for each major concept (or group of concepts), or to separate sub-topics, details, etc.
- While you are rereading your notes, be aware of how the information is organized and how you link it together to understand it.

STEP 7 ☞ Create a graphic organizer.

- Design a graphic organizer for this pile (see *Creating a Graphic Organizer* on page 119).
- Quickly reread each pile of notes to make sure all essential material is represented in the graphic organizer.

STEP 8 ☞ Repeat.

- Continue with Steps 6–7 for each remaining pile.
- Combine any of the graphic organizers where possible and appropriate.

Hint: *Design graphic organizers as a regular part of your study time, not just to study for a test. If you keep them current by continually adding information as you get it, you'll have more time to review when a test is announced and most of the information will already be in your memory!*

Why Create Graphic Organizers?

Graphic organizers are super tools to help you strengthen your brain power. They are very successful because they work with the way you learn and incorporate many positive aspects of what research tells us about learning. Creating graphic organizers the right way brings all your learning modalities together at once to produce a fantastic memory so you can recall facts when you need them. They allow you to use the most powerful learning tools for your brain all at once.

Graphic organizers allow you to:

● see the whole picture/end result and how concepts relate to each other or build on each other (right brain).

● see individual parts/details, how they are broken down to smaller parts, and how they work to make a whole (left brain).

● use colors, shapes, placement, and words/numbers (quick recognition and long-term factors).

● incorporate all the learning modalities (visual, auditory, and kinesthetic).

● HEAR IT—talk out loud to yourself all the time while studying (except when reading for speed).

● SEE IT—watch yourself while you write it.

● SAY IT—be aware of your thoughts as you say it out loud.

● WRITE IT—write the information so your mind will see the words and patterns.

● DO IT—be physically active by reorganizing the information from your notes onto another paper by condensing the information into a pattern.

● comprehend and memorize simple and complicated material easily.

● learn large amounts of material with greater recall.

● recreate these organizers from memory on test papers to greatly reduce stress, combat confusion, and provide direction for essays.

You can see how powerful these study tools can be to your learning. Study the *Sample: Pizza Graphic Organizer* on page 122 before constructing one of your own.

REMEMBER TO TALK OUT LOUD!

MATERIALS YOU WILL NEED:

- template with large and obviously different shapes (data processing template, etc., purchased at office supply stores) or you can simply draw your own shapes

- bright, different colored pencils or pens with small tips to clearly write words

- blank paper

- white-out/eraser

Steps to Creating a Graphic Organizer

See *Sample: Pizza Graphic Organizer* on page 122 as you follow these steps. (Also, refer to *Constructing Study Sheets* on page 117.)

STEP 1 ☞ Create one organizer for each "pile" in your dump and pile system.

STEP 2 ☞ Select one main category from your notes and/or handouts. Use the title on your 3" x 5" card on the pile of your study sheets.

STEP 3 ☞ Write the main topic at the center of your paper using one color of ink (see *Sample: Pizza Graphic Organizer* on page 122).

STEP 4 ☞ Take a major sub-topic and write it inside a simple shape off to the side of the main topic (use the color coding on your notes—see example: meat on pizza).

- Use one color for the main topic and a different color for each sub-topic shape and detail (do not use shades of the same color, or similar colors such as pink, red, or orange in the same organizer).

• Example (see *Sample: Pizza Graphic Organizer* on page 122)
Pizza (black ink); the rectangle and words: meat, pepperoni, sausage, Canadian bacon (red ink); the oval and words: green peppers, olive, mushrooms (green ink).

STEP 5 ☞ Use straight lines to write in details and connect them to the sub-topic shape (use the color coding on your notes--see example: pepperoni on pizza).

STEP 6 ☞ Repeat the previous two steps as many times as needed.

STEP 7 ☞ Remember to appropriately abbreviate all words.

Remember these simple rules:

● Your mind remembers colors, shapes, placement, words, and numbers in that order.

● Be an active learner: hear it, see it, say it, write it, and do it as you create graphic organizers.

● Combining any information into any form of graphic organizer helps your mind learn faster and remember longer.

● Use only two to three words per entry.

● Leave spaces; stay simple.

● Break down the material into small units; add 5–7 items at one time, study them, then add 5–7 more, etc.

● Create organizers often for every subject. Keeping current with information to be learned lowers stress, reduces test study time, and gives you a feeling of control!

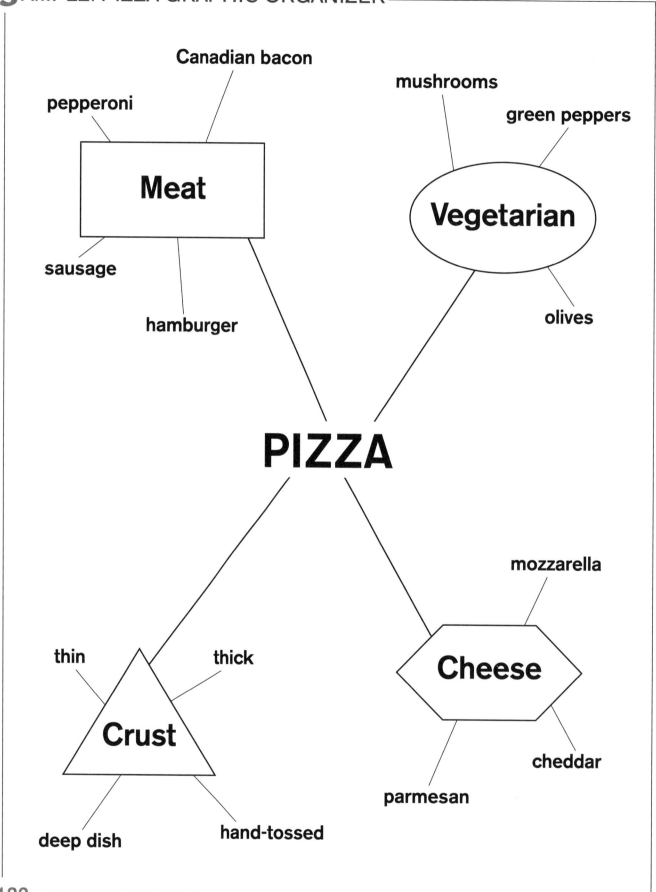

STEP 1 ☞ Study the graphic organizer carefully for 30 seconds with the intent of reproducing it immediately.

STEP 2 ☞ Turn the paper over and put aside.

STEP 3 ☞ Reproduce the organizer on a piece of unlined paper (printer paper) using pen/pencil, as fast (abbreviations help) and accurately as you can.

- Use colored pens/pencil so that your mind will link all the information together by color.

- Use blue/black ink or pencil to practice reproducing it to simulate a test situation where you cannot use color.

- Your mind will become accustomed to creating in color then reproducing in black and white.

STEP 4 ☞ Compare your reproduction to the original organizer.

STEP 5 ☞ Check for any incorrect placement or omission of concepts.

- Don't be too concerned if details are not in the exact location as the original organizer in relation to the sub-topic. What really matters is that they are grouped correctly with the right concept.

STEP 6 ☞ Correct any errors on the reproduction.

STEP 7 ☞ Study the original organizer again for 30 seconds.

STEP 8 ☞ Repeat Steps 2–7 until you can reproduce it correctly.

- If you do not make the attempt to completely reproduce the entire organizer again and only write in the correct answers from Step 6, the next time you reproduce this organizer (in the middle of a test) you will miss the same information.

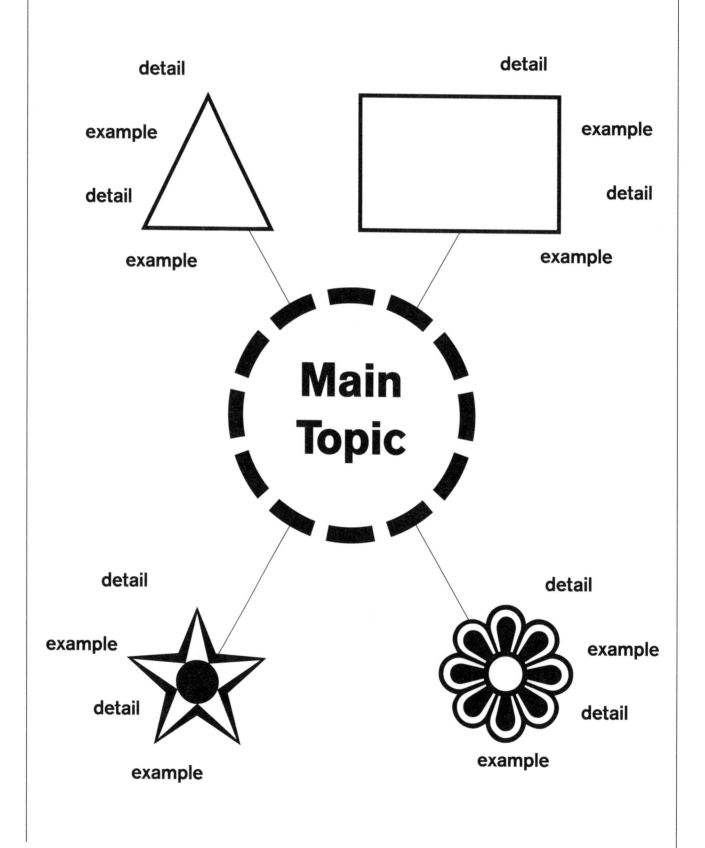

detail

example

detail

example

detail

example

detail

example

Main Topic

detail

example

detail

example

detail

example

detail

example

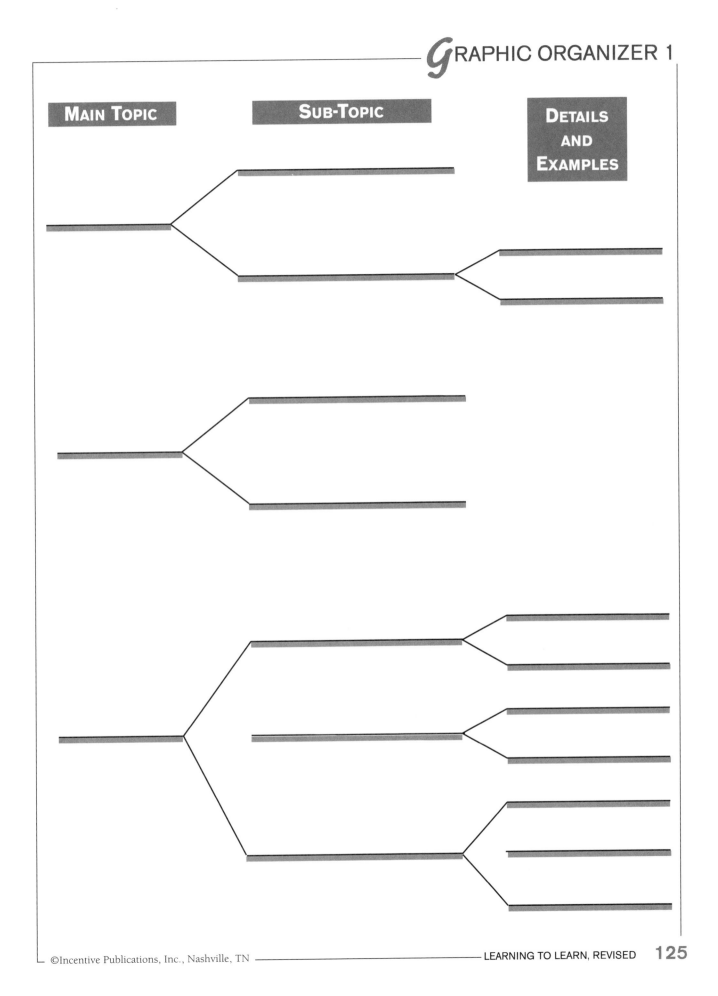

MAIN TOPIC

SUB-TOPIC

DETAILS AND EXAMPLES

MAIN TOPIC

Details

Examples

Examples

Examples

Details

Examples

Examples

Examples

Details

Examples

Examples

Examples

Details

Examples

Examples

Examples

Details

Examples

Examples

Examples

Sub-topic

Details

Examples

Examples

Examples

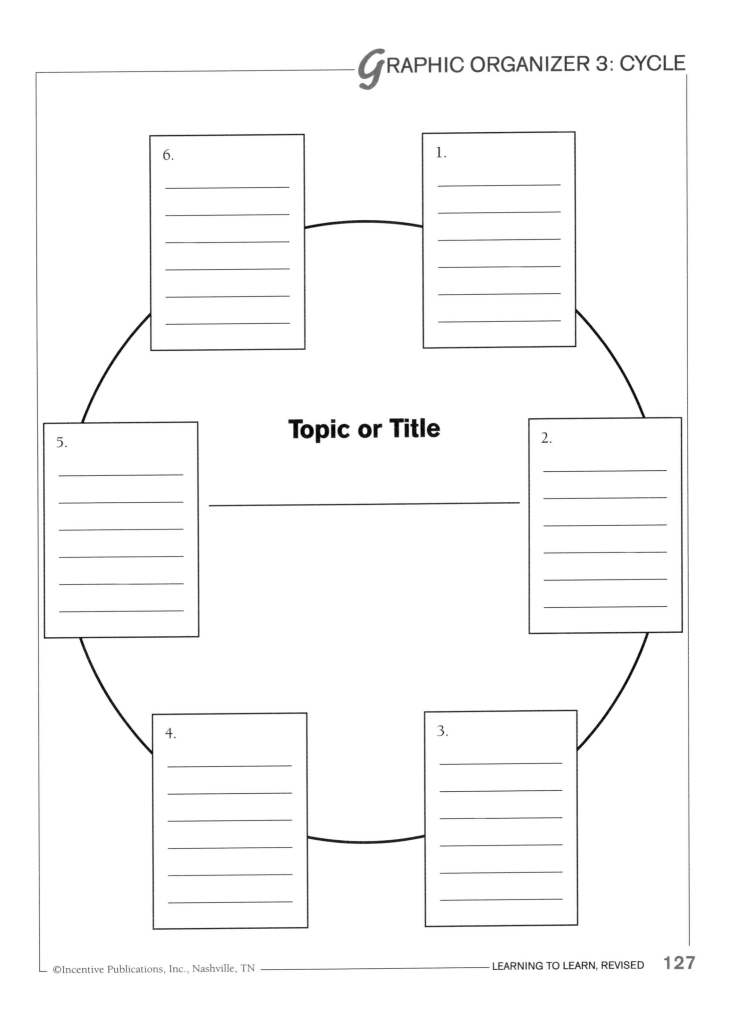

6.

1.

Topic or Title

5.

2.

4.

3.

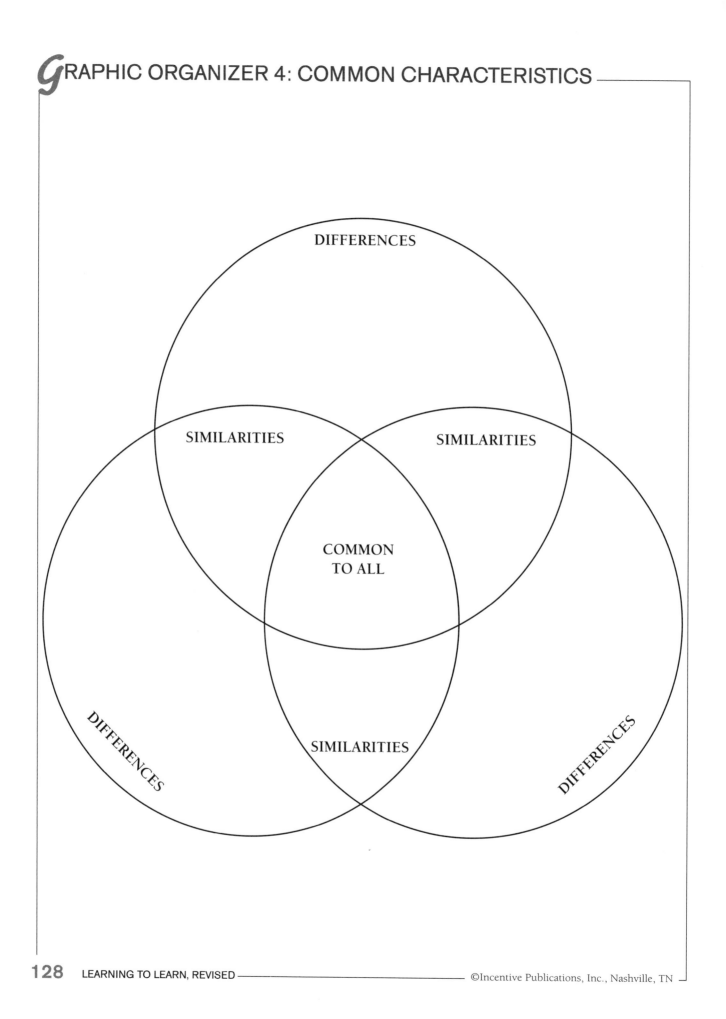

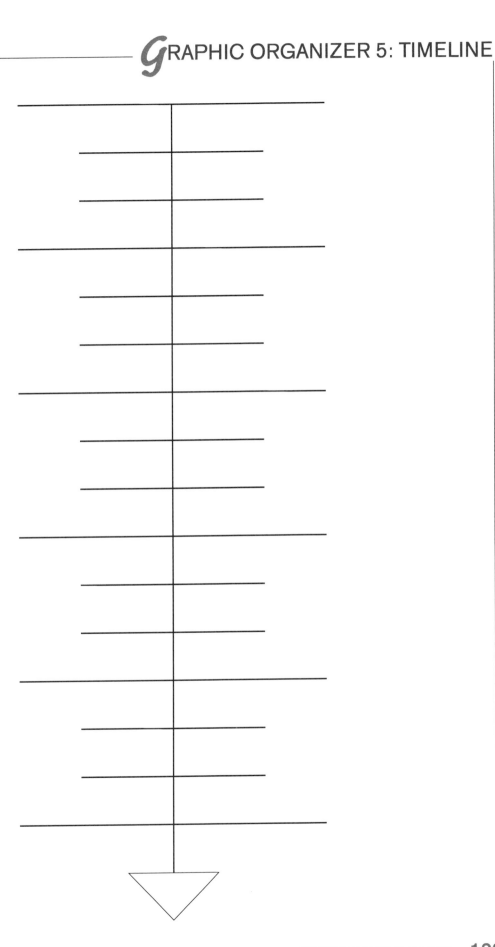

GRAPHIC ORGANIZER 6: TREE #1

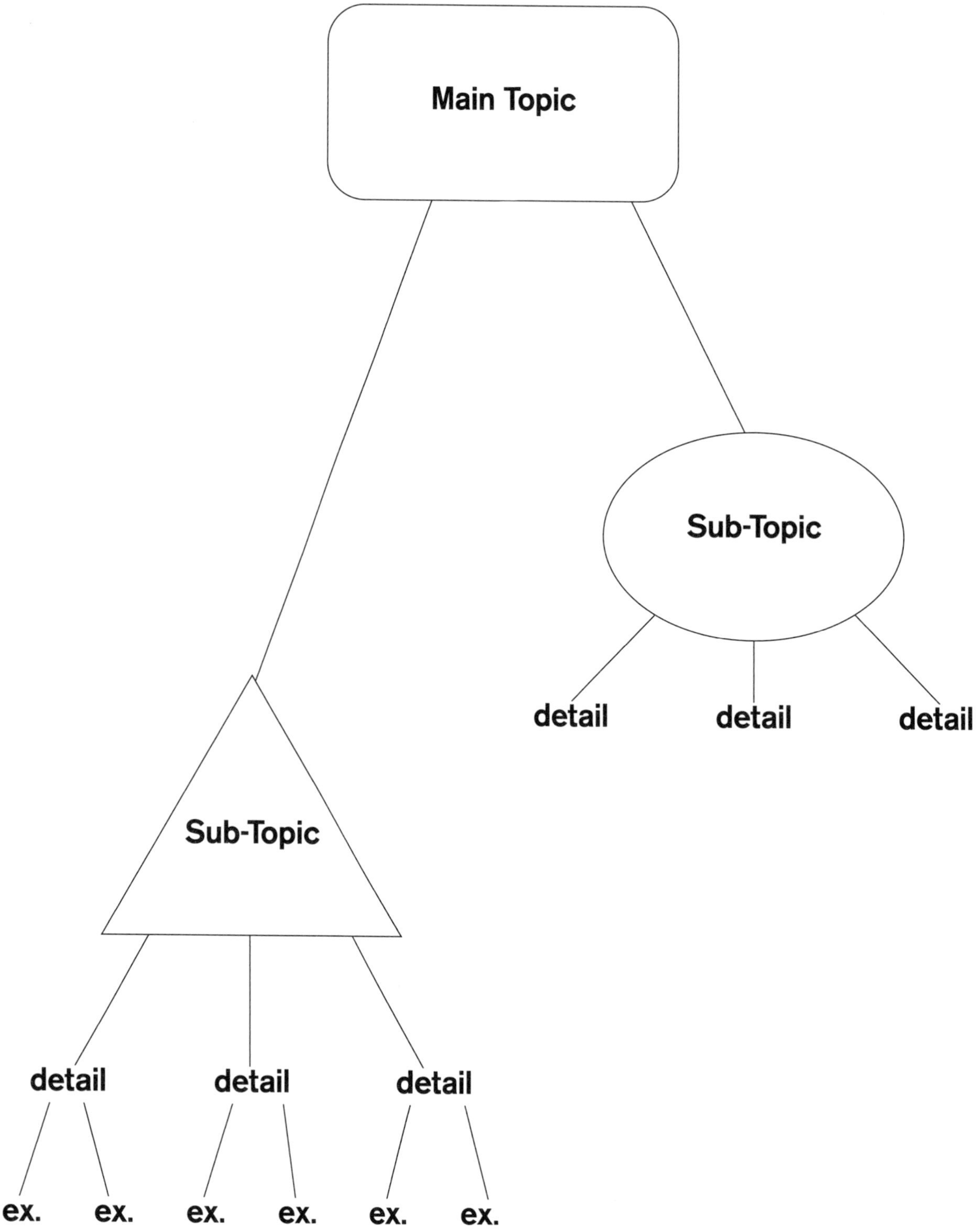

Main Topic
Sub-Topic
detail
detail
detail
Sub-Topic
detail
detail
detail
ex.
ex.
ex.
ex.
ex.
ex.

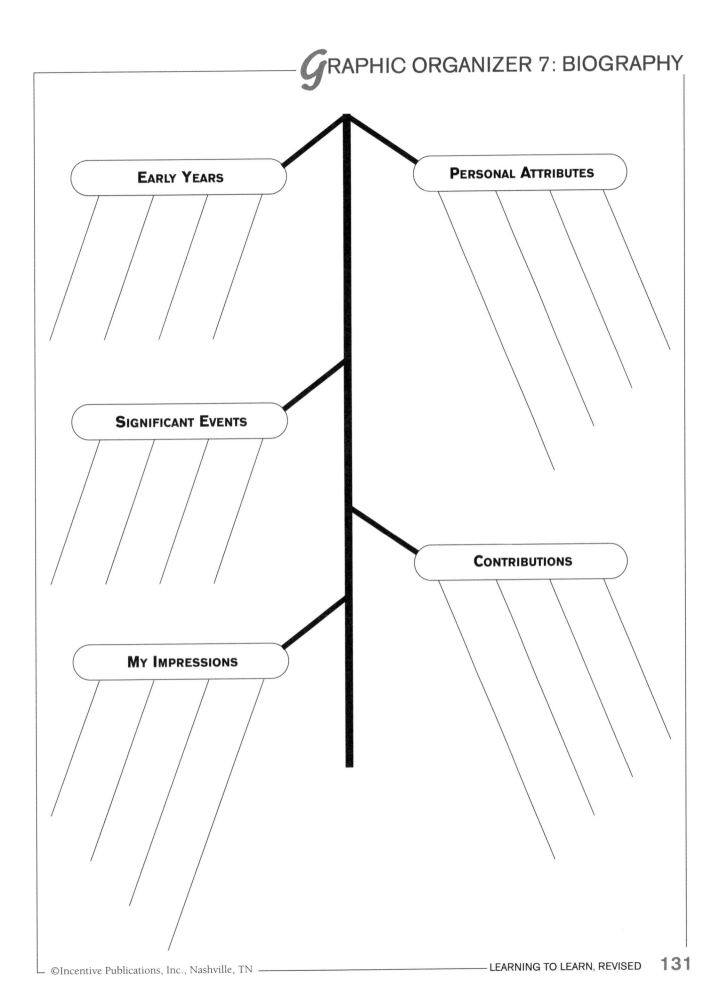

EARLY YEARS

PERSONAL ATTRIBUTES

SIGNIFICANT EVENTS

CONTRIBUTIONS

MY IMPRESSIONS

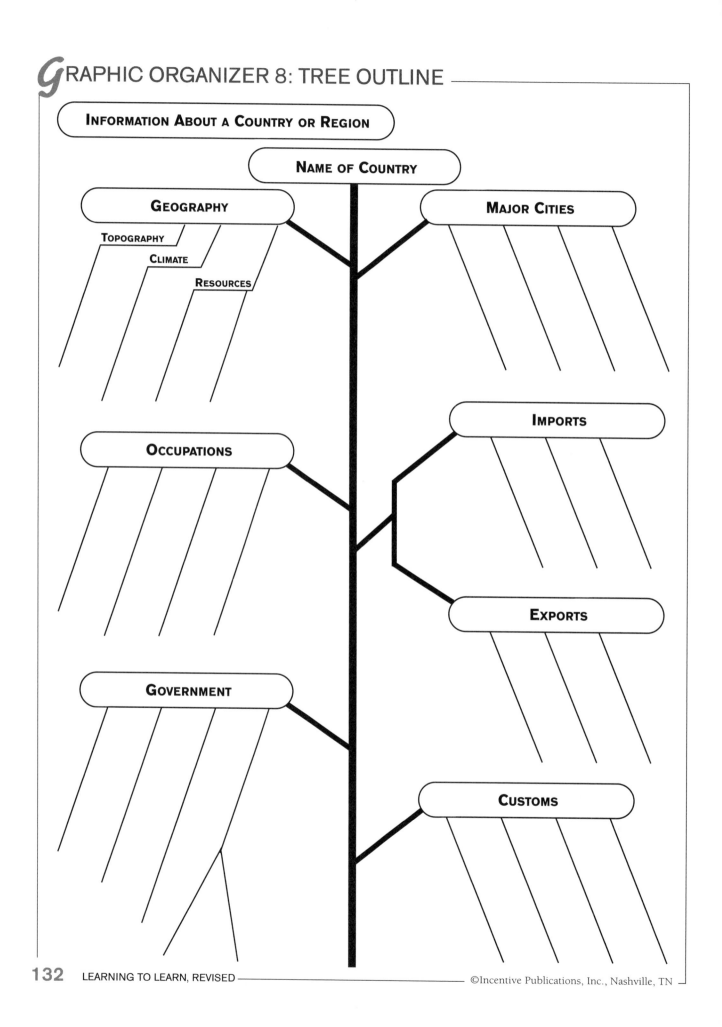

INFORMATION ABOUT A COUNTRY OR REGION

NAME OF COUNTRY

GEOGRAPHY

TOPOGRAPHY

CLIMATE

RESOURCES

MAJOR CITIES

IMPORTS

OCCUPATIONS

EXPORTS

GOVERNMENT

CUSTOMS

1. Read through the material.

2. Complete the chart.

3. Cover each side, one at a time, and quiz yourself.

Question	Answer
	Write answers here in your own words.
Who	
What	
How	
Where	
When	
Why	

Write one concept
or idea on
each card.

Key Words   **Code**
(Keyed to book,
study sheet, etc.)

One concept here.

Supporting details here.

Key Words   **Code**
(Keyed to book,
study sheet, etc.)

One concept here.

Supporting details here.

_____   _____

_____   _____

_____   _____

_____   _____

_____   _____

_____   _____

_____   _____

_____   _____

_____   _____

_____   _____

_____   _____

_____   _____

_____   _____

_____   _____

_____   _____

_____   _____

_____   _____

_____   _____

_____   _____

_____   _____

LITERATURE NOTE-TAKING METHOD

3" x 5" or 5" x 7" note cards

TITLE: **AUTHOR:**

SETTING:

CHARACTERS (3 to 5 adjectives for each)**:**

CONFLICT(S):

SPECIAL EFFECTS: **STORY LINE:**

REACTION:

TITLE: **AUTHOR:**

SETTING:

CHARACTERS (3 to 5 adjectives for each)**:**

CONFLICT(S):

SPECIAL EFFECTS: **STORY LINE:**

REACTION:

Topic Sentence:

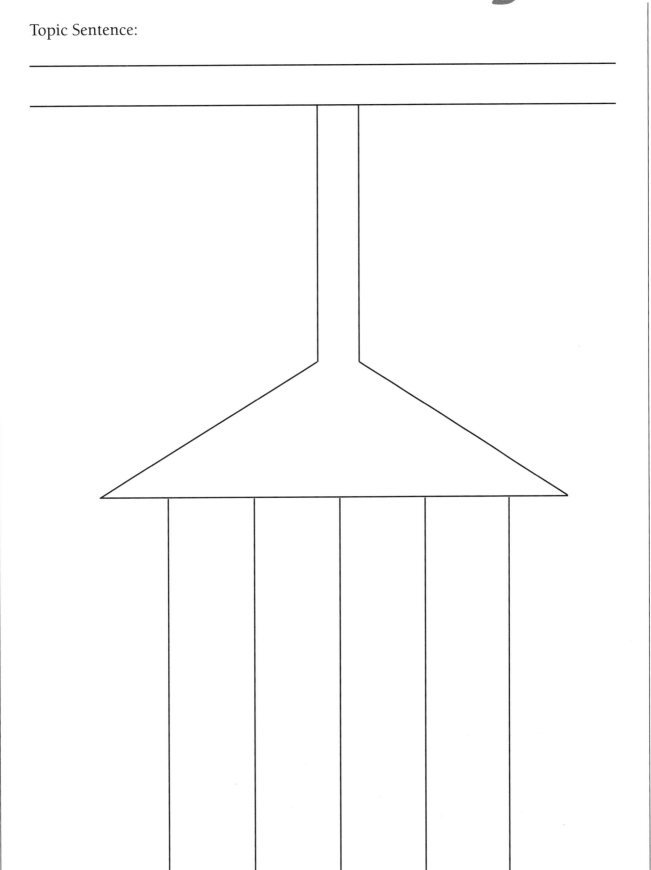

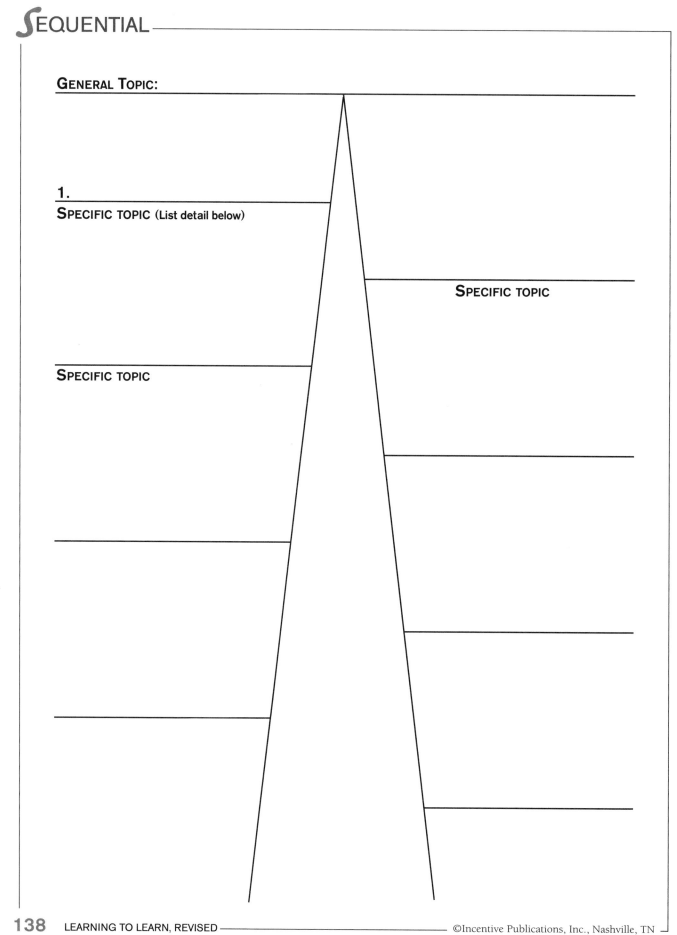

GENERAL TOPIC:

1.

SPECIFIC TOPIC (List detail below)

SPECIFIC TOPIC

SPECIFIC TOPIC

TOPIC SENTENCE:

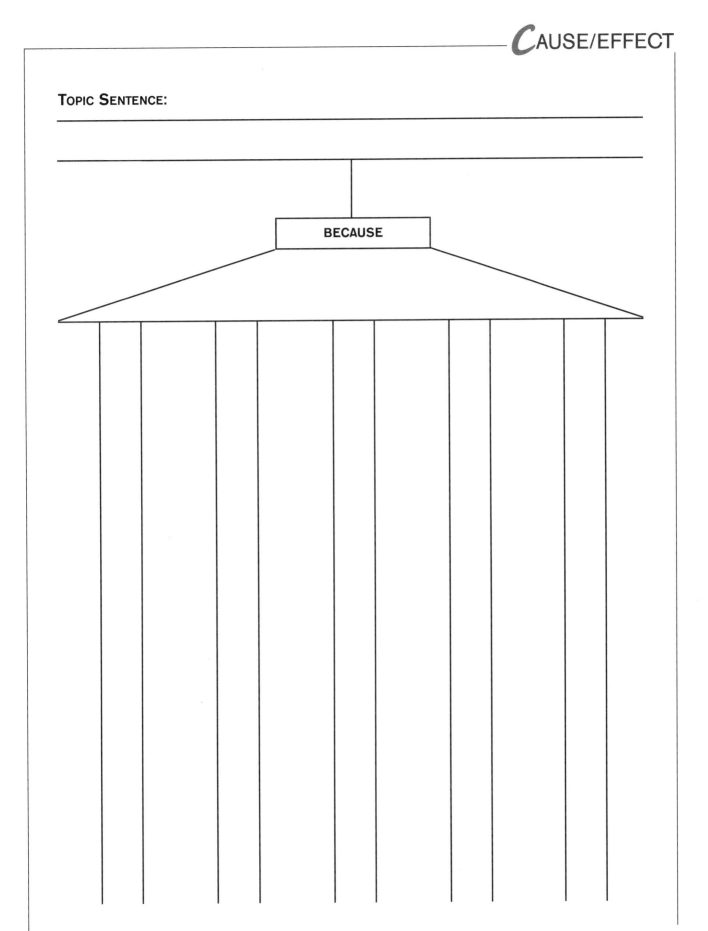

BECAUSE

COMPARISON/CONTRAST

TOPIC SENTENCE:

_____

_____

_____

SUBJECTS

↓   ↓

SIMILARITIES

_____

_____

_____

_____

_____

_____

_____

_____

↓   ↓

DIFFERENCES

_____

_____

_____

_____

_____

_____

_____

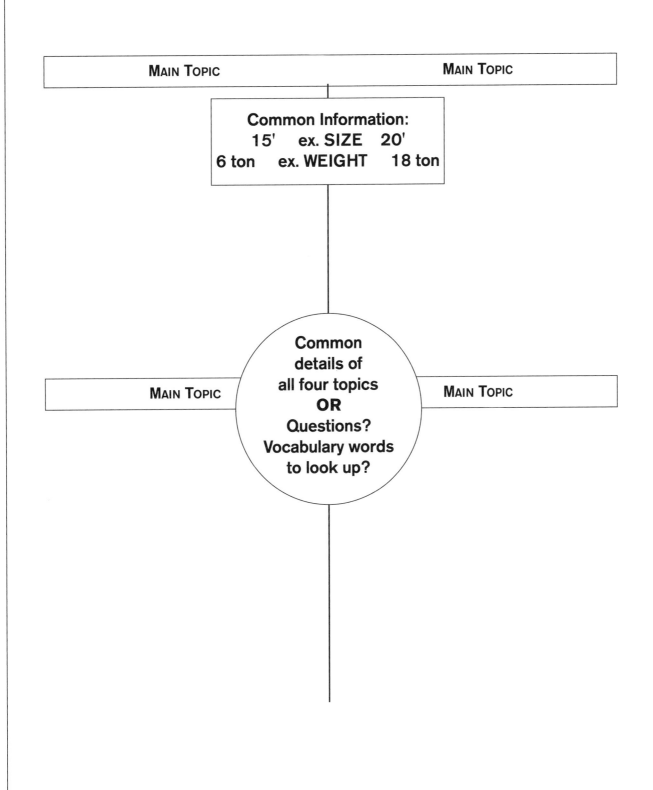

READING SKILLS

FOCUS ON
READING SKILLS

1. Determine reading purpose and rate before beginning.

2. Intend to remember what you read and take notes.

3. Use SQ3R.

4. Know your textbook and how to use it.

5. Learn to predict, clarify, and summarize.

6. Question while you read—read to answer the questions.

7. Read then recite what you read.

8. Discuss what you read.

9. Review what you already know about the topic before reading.

10. Watch for "signal words" that indicate main ideas and important details.

11. Remember the results of your learning styles assessment.

12. Choose reading tools that focus on your strengths and minimize your weaknesses.

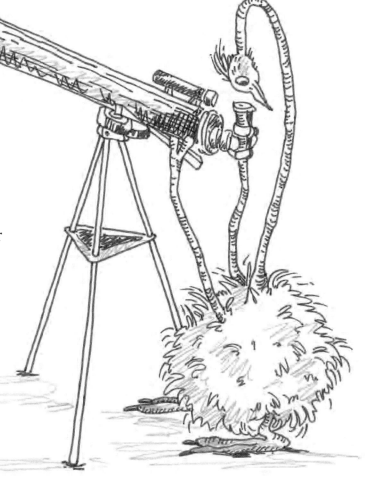

Reading is a primary source for gaining information and learning. Just as there are any number of ways and reasons to do anything, so it is with reading. To learn, apply, and master specific reading strategies is to make study time more efficient and effective. It is time well-spent. In fact, it is guaranteed to save you time in the long run.

There are numerous aids that you can use to increase your reading "brain power." Pre-reading techniques give you an "overview" and help you determine the importance of the materials as well as your purpose and rate for reading. Flexible reading habits lead to quality study skills and increased memory. Learning how to survey textbooks, skim, spot "signal words," find main ideas, check for comprehension, and read illustrations will improve your understanding and grades. So, give the following reading hints, tips, and methods a try, and soon they will become habits you'll want to keep.

As you review these reading techniques, focus on the elements that best fit your learning modality (visual, auditory, or kinesthetic).

A few suggested reading aids for the three modalities are:

VISUAL:	AUDITORY:	KINESTHETIC:
• Form pictures in your mind • See parts of words • Look for context clues	• Read aloud • Have discussions • Teach someone the new information	• Pace/walk as you read • Role play • Take notes after reading each paragraph

　　　　©Incentive Publications, Inc., Nashville, TN

There are many ways to do any one thing—many approaches to solving a problem, painting a picture, and achieving desired results. Reading for different purposes is no different. You probably would not read a newspaper in the same manner and with the same goal as you would read a science textbook. You would read a pamphlet about how to construct a bookshelf differently than you would a novel or short story.

It is very important that the purpose and kind of material be appropriate for your reading speed. First, determine the type of material you are going to read. Find out if it is:

- new information
- review material/information
- purely for enjoyment
- fiction
- nonfiction
- technical

Secondly, set your purpose for reading the selection by asking yourself:

"WHY AM I READING THIS?"

- for a test
- for enjoyment
- for the main ideas
- to discuss later
- to get an overall, general view

"WHAT IS MY END GOAL?"

- mastery of subject
- understanding the concept
- understanding the plot/characters

"WHAT AM I EXPECTED TO REMEMBER?"

- details
- author's mood, opinion, intent
- sequence of events
- cause/effect
- relationships

Once you clearly understand your goal and the type of reading material, match these with an appropriate reading rate (see page 149).

In summary

1. Determine type of material
2. Set purpose
3. Decide reading rate
4. Read

Strategy for Rate of Reading	Purpose	Materials
1. Scanning	1. To gain a sense of main topics and ideas; to get a clear picture of overall organization. Use to find a specific detail such as a date, name, country, answer to question, etc. Do not read all of the words.	1. dictionary; listings/lists; newspapers; magazine articles
2. Skimming	2. To find main ideas, cause/effect; to survey for general ideas. To recognize sequences and relationships between headings/sub-headings. To identify the topic. To look for italicized words/phrases. Use as "pre-reading" of more difficult materials. Do not read all of the words.	2. easy-to-read print; magazines; fiction; previewing texts
3. Rapid Reading	3. To read all of the words at a fast rate. To search for specific information.	3. same as #2—but read for main ideas and their details
4. Slow Reading	4. To find all of the available information. Take notes and/or underline.	4. any textbook to be read for details; technical articles
5. Careful Reading	5. To find procedures; to follow step-by-step instructions; to analyze and evaluate content. Take detailed notes or outline.	5. complex ideas or concepts; nonfiction, sequential/detailed reports; poetry, scientific data or texts

PURPOSE

As quickly as possible, selectively read the material to find specific information and to survey for general ideas.

WHEN

- You are not responsible for details or in-depth comprehension.
- You want/need a pre-reading exercise to familiarize yourself with the material.

WHY

- To avoid reading what you don't need to read.
- To save time.
- To get an overall view . . . in a hurry.
- To determine if you need to read further.

HOW

Do not read every word, just . . .

- Read main titles.
- Read subtitles—look for specific names, dates, lists, etc., in each paragraph.
- Glance at any illustrations, pictures, charts, etc.
- Read first and last sentences of each paragraph if time permits.
- Read the questions at the end of the paragraph/chapter.

Always know why you are skimming the material, and what specific things you are looking for in the material.

Main ideas help you to recognize and remember supporting details. They are the "topics" of entire paragraphs or selections. Main ideas often are found in first or last sentences and paragraphs, but they can be located anywhere within the material.

When trying to find the main idea:

● Determine what the topic of the paragraph is. "What is being discussed?"

● Determine what it says about the concept. "What is the author saying?"

● Make up a statement that would include all of the details.

● Check to see if the statement (main idea) covers only the information in that particular paragraph.

You also can find the main ideas in paragraphs by looking for the strategies authors choose to use in delivering their information, ideas, or concepts. They are:

first or last sentence............... important ideas stated in the opening or closing statements

examples................................... lists of specific traits, actions, and ideas that illustrate the main idea

comparison/contrast .... relating how something is alike or different from something else

vocabulary .... notice descriptive words and what one or two concepts they describe; look for italics and boldface type

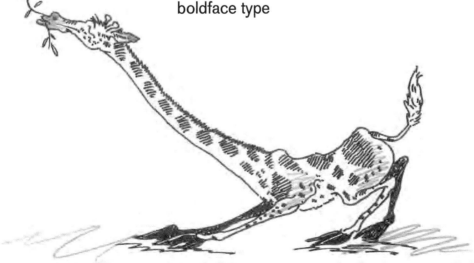

analogies........................... comparisons of the relationships of ideas, concepts, or things

figurative speech .... the use of one word or phrase to describe

reading between the lines...... what is not there but is implied

enumeration............................. listing of ideas

transition.................................. shows a change from one idea to another

descriptive................................ demonstrates how something looks, sounds, or feels

methodological .... tells how to do something; gives step-by-step directions

introductory.............................. may begin with questions and give definitions; signals the reader what the chapter is about

summary .... sometimes begins with "In summary" or "In conclusion"; is usually the last paragraph

definition .... used to qualify, describe, characterize, compare or contrast, give the limits of, or tell by anecdote

Signal words tell you what's coming and what to watch for as well as what you already have read. They may signal a list, summary, comparison/contrast, detail, main idea, beginning, or ending.

Watching for signal words as you skim or scan will immediately focus your attention or "signal" you to make note of the information to follow.

Listed below and on the next page are some signal words and their "meanings." Use context clues that improve reading ability.

READ ON—MORE IS COMING

and	first
more	second
moreover	third
furthermore	also
besides	finally
some	primarily
many	a key feature
for one thing	in addition
likewise	next
main	another

CONCLUSION/SUMMARY

therefore	hence
thus	as a result
finally	in summary
in conclusion	noteworthy
consequently	last of all

WORDS THAT ILLUSTRATE

for example
to illustrate
specifically
for instance
such as
following are

FOUR TYPES OF CONTEXT CLUES:

1. Definition—the easiest to use ("is, means . . .")

2. Comparison—unknown words compared with known words ("as, like . . .")

3. Contrast—opposite meaning ("but, not, however . . .")

4. Sense of Passage—the meaning in relation to other parts of the paragraph

REVERSE YOUR THINKING
yet
however
but
otherwise
nevertheless
still
in spite of
likewise
in contrast
instead
even though

WORDS OF IMPORTANCE
better	best
most	good
least	important
most of all	chief factor
above all	less
worst	bad
major	minor
all	some
few	

CAUSE/EFFECT WORDS
it is because
because
unless
as a result
effect
cause
the quality
attribute
for this reason
if
consequently
the result of which

WORDS THAT DEFINE
referred to as
is
the same as
means
termed
defined as
means the same
a synonym for

COMPARISON/CONTRAST WORDS
more	than
compares	nevertheless
otherwise	contrasts
differences	likeness
similar	similarly
alike	

Each time you receive a textbook that is new to you, take time to become acquainted with the parts of the book and how the teacher views the textbook.

Following are some questions which you may want to ask yourself as you look through the book.

Author or Authors

● Who wrote the book?

● What information is given about the author or authors?

● Did the author or authors write a section for the student?

● Does the book have a preface that explains how the book came to be written and how the book might be used?

Organization

● How is the book organized?

● What does the table of contents tell about the organization of the book?

● Is the organization historical, chronological, factual, or other?

● Does the book have chapters and/or units?

Timeliness

● When was the book written?

● Will the age of the book and its information be a problem in this class?

● Will you need to refer to other sources for more recent information?

From *Senior High Study Skills Booklet*, Jefferson County Schools, Colorado, © 1983. Used by permission.

Book Parts

- Does the book have a table of contents?
- Does the book have an index?
- Does the book have a glossary?
- Does the book have a bibliography?
- Does the book have an appendix or appendices?

More Organizational Points

- How are the various sections, units, and/or chapters organized?
- How is new vocabulary handled?
- Are new topics introduced in boldface type?
- Does the author include study questions?
- Does each section/chapter have an introduction and a summary?

Notes and Outlining

- What kind of notes will I need to take while reading the text?
- Can the sections be easily outlined?
- At what rate will I read and study this textbook?

Graphic Aids

- How are the illustrations handled in the book?
- Are graphic aids included such as graphs, charts, or tables?

From *Senior High Study Skills Booklet*,
Jefferson County Schools, Colorado, © 1983. Used by permission.

"Brain power" is significantly increased with the use of some type of "power reading strategy" or method. Like a finely tuned machine, your mind will work much more efficiently and effectively with a warm-up, rev-up, pace, and cool-down plan.

When you reuse a successful method of study consistently, your brain becomes accustomed to a specific pattern; therefore, you are able to increase your time effectiveness. By making a regular habit of successful study habits such as power reading strategies, studying should take less effort and time and should produce more focused, quality results. Additionally, these results are more likely to be permanent in your memory.

Be willing to give the following power reading strategy a try for three weeks—see whether it really makes a difference!

Step 1: Warmup

PREPARE YOUR GEAR

- Paper
- Pencil
- Notes
- Dictionary
- Texts
- 3" x 5" note cards

PREPARE YOUR SURROUNDINGS

- Find a place that is relatively quiet.
- Make sure there is good lighting.
- Sit in a comfortable chair.

PREPARE YOUR MIND

- Read to remember.
- Eliminate distractions.

REVIEW/REREAD THE ASSIGNMENT FOR CLARITY

- Refresh your memory.
- Determine your purpose for reading.
- Set/focus your mind on desired objectives and outcomes.
- Break down a complex reading assignment into reasonable "blocks."
  - ▲ Use paper clips or rubber bands to separate sections.
  - ▲ Consider subject headings/sub-headings.
  - ▲ Use the "estimated time" column on your assignment sheet (see *Use a Daily Assignment Sheet* on page 47) for the time needed to read the assignment. Add additional time for note taking.

SURVEY THE MATERIAL TO BE READ

- Use SQ3R system (see pages 162–165).
- Reflect on what you already know:
  - ▲ Relationships of material presented in class to the concepts in the text
  - ▲ New material presented in the text not covered in class
  - ▲ Main topics
  - ▲ Emphasized concepts
- Identify what's important—find the main ideas.

Adapted from a presentation by Peggy Isakson. Used by permission.

Step 2: Stretch Your Imagination

VISUALIZE YOURSELF DOING THE WORK

FORM QUESTIONS IN YOUR MIND
AND READ FOR THE ANSWERS

CONTINUALLY LINK CONCEPTS, IDEAS, AND INFORMATION
WITH WHAT YOU ALREADY KNOW

AFTER READING SEVERAL PARAGRAPHS
- Close the book.
- Recite from memory what you have just read.

TAKE OWNERSHIP OF THE MATERIAL BY RELATING IT
TO YOUR OWN EMOTIONS, EXPERIENCES, AND BELIEFS

Step 3: Consider Your Pace

CHOOSE YOUR PACE ACCORDING TO YOUR PURPOSE
- Review *Five Different Reading Rates* (page 149).
- Review *What Slows You Down—and How to Improve* (page 168).
- Become involved in your reading and set your purpose
  at the beginning.
- It is more effective/efficient to read groups of words and
  short phrases for ideas rather than reading word-by-word.
- Continue to read when you come to unfamiliar words.
  - ▲ It slows you down to look up words at this time.
  - ▲ You lose your "train of thought."
  - ▲ Often you can derive meaning through context clues.
- Look up unfamiliar words after finishing the paragraph.
  - ▲ Flag the word or write it on a 3″ x 5″ card.
  - ▲ Write a brief definition.

Adapted from a presentation by Peggy Isakson. Used by permission.

FOCUS/CONCENTRATE 30–45 MINUTES PER READING SESSION

TAKE A 10–15 MINUTE BREAK TO DO SOMETHING ACTIVE

Step 4: Pump Your Mind

STRETCH/WALK AROUND TO GIVE YOURSELF "THINKING POWER" ENERGY

WHEN YOUR MIND GETS OFF TRACK

- Make a check mark with a pencil on a piece of scratch paper.
  - ▲ This causes you to refocus your thinking.
  - ▲ Try to make fewer checks during the next reading block.
- Invent images as you read.
- Use your fingers to "guide" over subject headings.
- Talk to yourself while skimming and scanning if possible.

WHILE READING

- Read favorite/easier materials first—then more difficult materials.
- If your purpose is to take notes, See *SQ3R* on page 162.
  - ▲ Select and consistently use one method of note taking.
  - ▲ Read the information in short "blocks" that deal with the same topic, then quickly reread the information and take notes.

TAKE COMPLETE NOTES (BUT ONLY NECESSARY NOTES) AND INCLUDE

- Vocabulary words/definitions
- Words/phrases in italics
- Important names, dates, places
- Causes/effects
- Relationships between/among concepts

Adapted from a presentation by Peggy Isakson. Used by permission.

- Listed items
- Chapter headings, sub-headings and important supporting details
- Important information from charts, graphs, tables
- Note that supplement and add to your class notes

CONSTRUCT A MIND MAP

- Continue to add to it as you read.
- Actively organize your thoughts about the assignment.

USE A SYSTEM TO "FLAG" CONCEPTS (BY PARAGRAPHS)

- Color code ideas or write in margins where possible.
  - ▲ Green or U = understand
  - ▲ Yellow or C = confusing
  - ▲ Red or D = don't understand
- Use a pencil to write a code in the margins, and erase when you have finished with the text (for textbooks in which you cannot write).

Step 5: Cool Down and Review

SIT BACK AND RELAX FOR TWO MINUTES AND RECITE THE MAIN IDEAS ALOUD

CHOOSE/USE A MEMORY TECHNIQUE/MNEMONIC DEVICE

SHARE IDEAS WITH FAMILY OR FRIENDS

CONSTRUCT

- Study sheets
- 3" x 5" cards
- Graphic organizers (mind maps)

Adapted from a presentation by Peggy Isakson. Used by permission.

There are many study methods that can be used effectively and can be applied to textbook reading assignments. These methods are important and can save you time in the long run because they give you an overall view of the content as well as focus your mind on the purpose at hand.

You can gain much by understanding main ideas and concepts from the very beginning. Pre-reading exercises (such as "Survey" and "Question") as well as ending exercises (such as "Recite" and "Review") result in increased reading rates and comprehension. Finding, understanding, and applying main ideas and supporting details are much easier when a "power reading" approach is utilized. Also, committing information to memory is aided by such a systematic approach.

Having a "plan of attack" or study method that is used on a regular basis will guarantee success.

SQ3R was originally developed by Francis P. Robinson. It has been thoroughly researched, tested, and used widely as one of the best study skills for textbook reading. Using it the first time may prove to be a little time-consuming. However, as you continue to apply it, you'll find it to be one of the most efficient and effective study skills for increasing your brain power!

Survey

- Review the reading assignment.
- Read main headings/titles.
  - Look for larger type, capitalized, colored ink, boldface type, italicized type
  - Ask yourself, "What do I already know about this?"
  - Ask yourself, "How do these relate to each other?"
- Read sub-headings/titles.
  - Look for smaller type, underlined, italicized, capitalized, set in from margins
  - Ask yourself, "What do I already know about this?"
  - Ask yourself, "How do these relate to each other?"
- Notice vocabulary words/phrases in italics, boldface type, colored ink, and underlined type.
- Skim illustrations, charts, graphs, pictures, diagrams, listing of items or terms.
- Determine the general idea of the overall content.
- Read the questions at the end of the unit and/or chapter to load your mind with a purpose to read for the answers.
- Read any summary information at the end of the unit and/or chapter.

Question

- Turn main/sub-topics in boldface type into questions (use who, what, when, where, or why).
- Take any unanswered questions to class after completing the reading assignment.

Read

- Actively read and become involved.
- Always read aloud (except when reading a short story, novel, etc.).
- Read one paragraph at a time focusing on comprehension to find:
  - Main topic
  - Sub-topic
  - Details/examples
- Note sequence/order, if important.
- Visualize as you read—make it real.

Recite

- At the end of each paragraph, recall the main ideas aloud.
- Talk to yourself while you take appropriate notes (see *Text Note Taking* on page 101).
- Include cue phrases for your memory.
- Place your hand over your notes and try to recite the notes from that paragraph.
- Talk aloud while creating vocabulary flash cards on any new words presented in that paragraph (see *The Magic of Flash Cards* on page 112).
- Read the next paragraph, then take notes repeating these steps.
- Ask yourself, "How do the main topics, sub-topics, details/examples relate to each other?"

Review

- Scan your text notes.
- Reread questions at the end of the unit/chapter.
  Can you answer every one completely?
- Quiz yourself by using only the Key Words and talking aloud to recite as many sub-topics and related details/examples you can remember (see *Sample: Note-Taking Form* on page 99).
- Ask yourself good study/review questions (see *Thinking . . . Odds and Ends* on page 269).
- Review flash cards just before you go to sleep
- Make study sheets (see *Constructing Study Sheets: Dump & Pile System* on page 117).
- Create a graphic organizer (see *Creating a Graphic Organizer* on page 119).

Use this chart to monitor your SQ3R practice. Use it consistently until it becomes a habit. You should see a decrease in "amount of time spent" each time you use the SQ3R chart. Give it a try—you won't regret it!

Assignment	Due Date ___ Amount of time spent ___ Class	Due Date ___ Amount of time spent ___ Class	Due Date ___ Amount of time spent ___ Class	Due Date ___ Amount of time spent ___ Class	Due Date ___ Amount of time spent ___ Class	Due Date ___ Amount of time spent ___ Class	Due Date ___ Amount of time spent ___ Class	Due Date ___ Amount of time spent ___ Class	Due Date ___ Amount of time spent ___ Class	Due Date ___ Amount of time spent ___ Class
SURVEY										
QUESTION										
READ										
RECITE										
REVIEW										

IMPORTANT COMPREHENSION SKILLS

Ask yourself the following questions to know if you have comprehended your reading assignment.

COMPREHENSION—*a summary; the capacity for understanding and gaining knowledge.*

1. Can I make good sense of the information?

2. Can I summarize the information in my own words and give it a title?

3. Did my reading rate match my purpose?

4. What was the main idea? Can I find a general statement supported by details?

5. Can I recite any details? How do they fit into the whole?

6. Is there anything I don't understand?

7. Can I identify and define the vocabulary in context? How does it relate to the topic?

8. Can I draw any conclusions from the information presented? How does this relate to what I am reading?

9. Do I understand the sequence in which the events occurred? How does one concept build upon another?

10. Can I make an inference based on the given facts?

11. Can I predict an outcome?

12. Can I recognize the author's tone of the message he/she is trying to get across?

13. Did I summarize in writing after each paragraph I read?

14. Can I teach this material to someone else?

Knowing how to "read" graphic illustrations such as charts, tables, and graphs is a matter of following a few steps. Keep in mind that the purpose of graphics is to demonstrate comparisons/contrasts, changes, trends, outcomes, or explanations.

HOW TO APPROACH GRAPHICS

- Read the title, subtitle, heading, or sub-headings.
  - helps focus your mind on the purpose
  - gives overview of information

- Read directional words/phrases on all sides.
  - introduces/explains the vocabulary
  - provides directions and explanations
  - gives information as to what units the chart represents (time, money, mathematical units, etc.)

- Read the graphic illustration.
  - watch for details, relationships
  - be aware of codes (numerical, color, symbols)
  - be aware of the general, overall concept

- Draw conclusions.
  - predict patterns
  - analyze relationships
  - note what caused the change, increase, decrease
  - predict the next step (not shown) on the graph
  - study how each part fits into the whole

TYPES OF GRAPHICS

- Diagrams use pictures, symbols, lines, and labels to show location of parts, and how they relate to each other to construct the whole.
  - line diagrams use labels, arrows/lines, symbols, and pictures to demonstrate how things work
  - picture diagrams use pictures (cross sections or cutaways) and labels to demonstrate location and how the parts make a whole

- Graphs show pictures of information.
  - bar graphs use columns of bars to demonstrate how things compare
  - line graphs use lines to demonstrate change
  - pie graphs use circles and pie slices to demonstrate relationships of parts to a whole

- Maps show location and relationships of parts to the whole.
  - numerous types: general road and state maps, bus routes, regional and district maps, weather maps, political and geological boundary maps, etc.

- Tables show how parts relate to one another or to the whole through use of words, names, and numbers.
  - numerous types: schedules, mileage, statistics

REASONS FOR POOR READING	HELPFUL SOLUTIONS

1. Lack of purpose

2. Inappropriate reading rate

3. Poor vision

4. Eye stress/strain

1. Intend to "read to learn."

   Use SQ3R on page 162.

   Refer to *Determining Reading Purpose* (page 147).

2. Be flexible according to your specific purpose—refer to *Five Different Reading Rates* (page 149).

3. Have your eyes checked by a doctor.

4. Have your eyes checked by a doctor.

   Place your desk light above reading material but below eye level.

   Check for appropriate lighting.

   Rest your eyes periodically.

   Clean your glasses/contacts.

   Get up and walk around.

   Don't bend your neck.

   Hold your book upright at a 45-degree angle and at a proper distance.

5. Regressive reading
   (Rereading words and sentences again and again)

5. Train your eyes to move ahead smoothly at a fixed pace and rhythm. Use your finger or index card if you have to for a short period of time. Set a purpose for reading at the very beginning. Read for:
   • main topic
   • sub-topics
   • details/examples

REASONS FOR POOR READING	HELPFUL SOLUTIONS

6. Inappropriate eye movement (Skip words/phrases; skip lines or focus on wrong line)

6. Use your finger, ruler, or 3″ x 5″ card to help your eyes track. Do not make this a habit, but use it only to establish an eye movement pattern.

7. Word-by-word reading (Too slow)

7. Train your eyes to "see" phrases instead of single words:
   - Begin slowly by widening your visual "spread" to group words.
   - Make a conscious effort to pace yourself.
   - Keep increasing the length to include many words.
     Try to force your eyes to move smoothly and rhythmically instead of jerking.
   - Listen to a clock tick and pace yourself.

REASONS FOR POOR READING

HELPFUL SOLUTIONS

8. Lack of concentration (daydreaming)

8. Record your concentrated reading time and consistently try to increase it. Have a positive attitude that you can improve. When you notice your mind wandering, make a check mark on a piece of paper to refocus your thoughts. Try to decrease the number of marks each time you read.

9. Lack of confidence

9. Stop thinking of yourself as a slow or poor reader. Know and believe that there are many ways you can use to improve. Have patience with yourself. Make reading a natural habit. Convince yourself that reading will become easier and more fun with practice. Brainstorm what you already know about the topic before you begin reading it. Know that there is important information to be gained from reading the assignment.

REASONS FOR POOR READING		HELPFUL SOLUTIONS
10. Poor Posture		10. Sit up and do not bend your neck. Use proper position, angle, and distance for books. Use a good desk chair.
11. Moving your head instead of your eyes to read		11. Cup your chin with your hand and put your elbow on the table/desk. When you feel your head move, it will remind you of your habit.

1. Know your purpose before you read.

2. Read to remember.

3. Skip what you don't need to read.

4. Read for ideas and continually take notes after reading each paragraph.

5. Read for the knowledge of the information rather than for decoding skills (sounding out words one-by-one).

6. Read the first and last sentence of each paragraph for main ideas and summary.

7. Question while you read and read to answer the questions.

8. Guess what the author is trying to tell you.

9. Have a plan for how to read the subject matter.

10. Read the questions at the end of the chapter or section first. They usually reflect/signal the main ideas of the material to be read.

DID YOU KNOW...

- After a single reading, the average student forgets 80% of what has been read.

- Research has shown that students who spend 25% of their time reading and 75% of their time reciting what they have read retain much more of the information than those who spend 100% of their time reading.

Try these hints:

● Reread the material and put each sentence into your own words after reading it.

● Change your surroundings, move around, and become physically active.

● Try to visualize and feel the concept or information.

● Build and understand the paragraph by reading one sentence at a time.

● Build and understand the reading assignment by fully comprehending one paragraph before moving on to the next.

● Form a study group.

● Read the material aloud and in front of a mirror if possible.

● Decrease your reading rate.

● Summarize at the end of each paragraph by writing or reciting.

● Discuss the material with a family member or friend.

● Put the book down for awhile and return to it in 30 minutes.

● Ask the teacher for help or get a tutor.

● Pretend that you understand the material and try to teach it to someone else.

● Look up alternative references in the library.

MEMORY

FOCUS ON

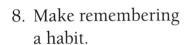EMORY

1. Link whatever you're trying to learn with what you already know.

2. Intend to remember when you learn.

3. Use mnemonics that work for you.

4. Colors, shapes, placement, and pictures are important to your memory.

5. Get past short-term memory and learn for long-term memory.

6. Make your memorizing methods organized.

7. Be smart—work with your memory, not against it.

8. Make remembering a habit.

9. Clarify, categorize, organize, and review information for better memory.

10. Break up material into small units and review daily.

11. Remember the results of your learning styles assessment.

YOUR MEMORY

Your mind is built to remember. It never forgets or loses anything throughout your entire life unless you suffer some type of brain injury or damage. When we say we "forget," actually we have lack of recall due to memory blocks or the misplacement of information.

It is a natural tendency to remember only those things or concepts with which we agree or deem important. We simply pay more attention to the ideas and information we intend to remember or can relate to our own priorities or experiences.

There are many techniques, strategies, mnemonics, and tricks which can enable you to memorize and recall almost anything. Most importantly, you must *intend* to remember and learn the information, then set a realistic goal. Realize that you can improve your memory. Don't waste time making excuses or blaming yourself. Use that time to your own advantage!

As you review these memory techniques, focus on the elements that best fit your learning modality: visual, auditory, or kinesthetic.

A few suggested memory aids for the three modalities are:

VISUAL:	AUDITORY:	KINESTHETIC:
• Use flash cards • Use acrostics • Reproduce graphic organizers from memory	• Make and use tapes • Talk aloud when reviewing • Set the information to music/use word links	• Physically "do it" • Focus all your senses on new information • Watch lips move in front of a mirror

 ©Incentive Publications, Inc., Nashville, TN

What Affects Memory

- How you receive, store, and retrieve information
- The context in which information is presented
- Your motivation for remembering
- Your stress level

Three Basic Processes Involved in Memory

encoding – the process of readying information for storage

storage – the saving of information for use in the future (memory)

retrieval – recalling information from storage (continuous process)

Six Types of Memory

1. Sensory Memory: fleeting impressions usually involving the five senses
   - taste
   - sound
   - smell
   - feel
   - sight

2. Motor Skill Memory: usually involving physical movement
   - riding a bicycle
   - swimming

3. Verbal/Semantic Memory: usually involving language
   - associated with the meaning of words or mathematical symbols

4. Photographic Memory: remembering visual information
   - picture memory
   - usually lasts only a short period of time

5. Short-Term Memory: temporary storage of selected memory items; any thoughts/experiences in the mind at any specific point in time
   - spelling words for the week
   - melodies to popular songs
   - license plate numbers
   - cramming for a test

6. Long-Term Memory: usually permanent storage of large amounts of material; unlimited in capacity for indefinite periods of time
   - your name, address, etc.
   - decoding skills that enable you to read
   - birthdays
   - foreign languages

Important Factors for Restoring Information in Long-Term Memory

- whether or not you intend to remember
- how meaningful the information is to you
- how the information is organized
- how easily the information can be linked with previous knowledge
- how learning blocks are spaced
- which mnemonic strategies are used
- if there is integration of the five senses

1. Learning stays with you. In order to forget something, you first have to learn it. You can't forget anything you don't learn or understand.

2. The human mind can remember five to seven unrelated ideas for a short time.

3. It takes about 15 to 25 minutes of practice over several days to successfully memorize and retain information.

4. Freud concluded that motivation, desire, and emotion play a large part in your "brain power."

5. With the exceptions of disease, injury, and death, the brain never forgets anything. Only our own inability to recall stands in our way.

6. The average adult cannot remember 50% of what he or she has just read. 24 hours later, recall is about 20%. Quick and constant review is the remedy.

7. For most people, visual information is processed in the right hemisphere of the brain, and verbal information is processed in the left hemisphere. If you make up a picture to go with material to be processed, it is then implanted in both hemispheres. This increases the chances of recall.

8. At least 40% of total learning time should be spent reviewing new information.

9. Adult attention spans average from 10 to 30 minutes.

10. We forget new information rapidly at first (if not rehearsed or practiced), but the rate of forgetfulness "levels off" over time.

11. Brain research suggests that information or thoughts create paths in the memory. These consistent paths are called "neural traces." By using and reusing the information through review, these nueral paths are deepened—which allows for easier and quicker recall of the information.

12. Effective memory is the ability to produce the right information at the right time.

13. Your brain remembers:

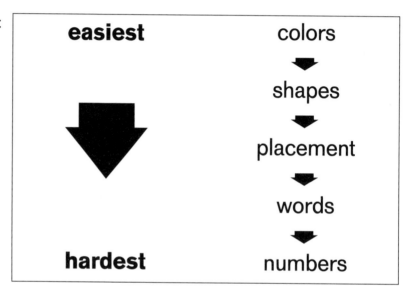

easiest

hardest

colors

shapes

placement

words

numbers

14. An effective memory:
   ● increases your adaptability and creativity
   ● finds relationships between new information and what is known
   ● improves with consistent use
   ● is essential to learning

15. Most of us forget more than 99% of the phone numbers we learn and more than 90% of the names of the people we meet.

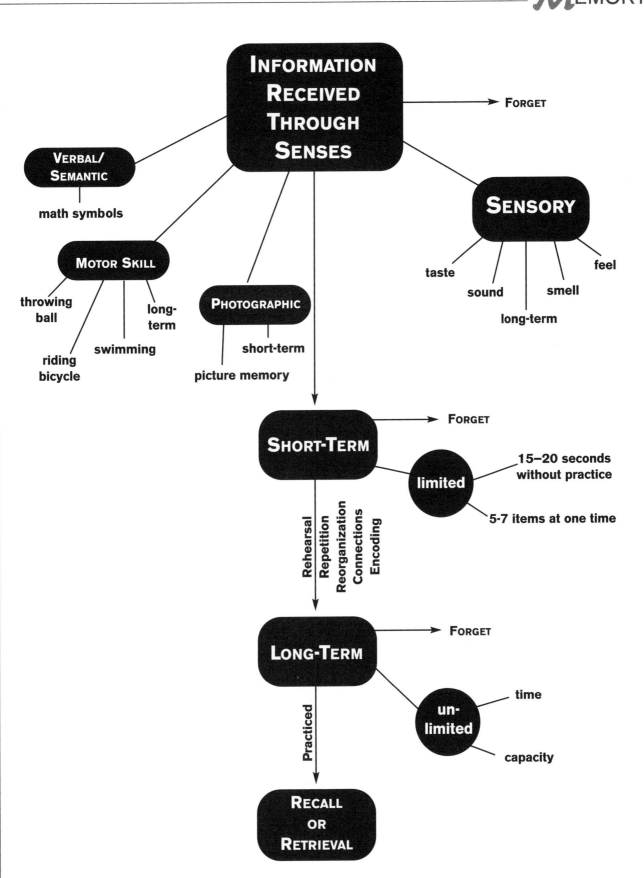

Memory traps are any factors that interfere with your ability to recall facts.

Why Do We Forget?

- lack of intentional purpose to remember
- faulty recall system
- poor listening
- lack of attention
- too painful or embarrassing to remember
- lack of preparation
- tired
- cannot recall because of misplaced data in the memory
- fear
- critical of information
- jump to conclusions
- physical stress or strain
- distracting
- boredom
- disliking the person or disagree with what he or she says
- lack of understanding
- mental stress or strain

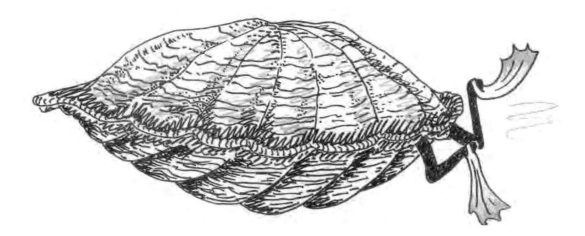

INTEND TO REMEMBER

● Don't bury yourself in excuses. See *Eliminating Excuses* on page 39.

● Become an active learner and create an interest for yourself.

 ■ Talk with others.

 ■ Get outside help.

 ■ Read critically.

 ■ Anticipate/predict outcomes or the sequence of events.

 ■ Make connections with known information.

 ■ See relationships.

 ■ Integrate the new idea with previous learning.

 ■ Be sure your mind stores the information your eyes see.

● Be positive.

 ■ You create your own boredom.

 ■ Your attitude can unlock your ability to recall.

 ■ Tell yourself "I will remember this!"

 ■ New learning can be frustrating. Be tolerant of yourself and the material.

● Pay attention by asking yourself:

 ■ "How do I remember?"

 ■ "What techniques/methods already are successful?"

 ■ "What do I remember about this?"

 ■ "What's important about this?"

 ■ "How will I use this?"

● Work with your memory—not against it.

 ■ Relax to allow better recall.

 ■ Let go of tension-blocking devices.

 ▲ Try to recall information related to blocked thought.

 ▲ Create visual images.

Organize

- Understand the material well.

- Decide how much to memorize at one time. Break it down into smaller units.

- Decide on memory strategy (mnemonics).

- Categorize material into meaningful units.

- Associate the material with other learned material.

- Learn material from the general to the specific.

Set a Goal to Learn and Remember

- Relate the information to your needs and goals—make it meaningful.

- Be realistic.

- Intend to apply the information to your life and make it familiar and comfortable to use.

Schedule Your Study Time

- Memory study is best distributed over several short periods/blocks of time to increase the amount of recall. Review often.

- Study the hardest material during prime study time.

Decide to Improve Your Concentration

● Eliminate distractions by considering:

- The place you study

- The time of day you study

- Your physical condition

- Background noise

● Focus your attention by:

- Setting a specific goal

- Timing yourself

- Becoming interested

- Varying the use of your skills and the difficulty of the material/subjects

- Finding a specific point of interest (watch, ring, fingers) to stare at while recalling/retrieving information

- Keeping a distractions list

    ▲ Add any distractions that break your concentration.

    ▲ Continually work toward reducing items on the list.

- Giving yourself rewards consistently and appropriately

When to Review

- Review after class to reinforce short-term memory.
- Review that evening just before going to sleep (uses the subconscious to continue processing information and aids long-term memory).
- Review while editing your notes within 24 hours.
- Review each day thereafter for 10 minutes each time.
- Review again in one month—immediately before going to sleep.
- Continually quiz yourself and try to relate previously learned materials to current studies.

Use What You Remember

- Apply the information.
  - Continually relate the new information with the known information.
  - If a portion of the information gets blocked from recall, retrieving associated material will often unblock the wanted information.

"Overlearn" the Material

- Continue to review even after you feel you know the information.
- Use the buddy system—find another student in your class with whom to discuss the material.

Reward Yourself

- Compliment yourself on a job well done.
- Learn to trust your memory—it is your best resource.

**Make Remembering
a Habit . . .**

PRACTICE!

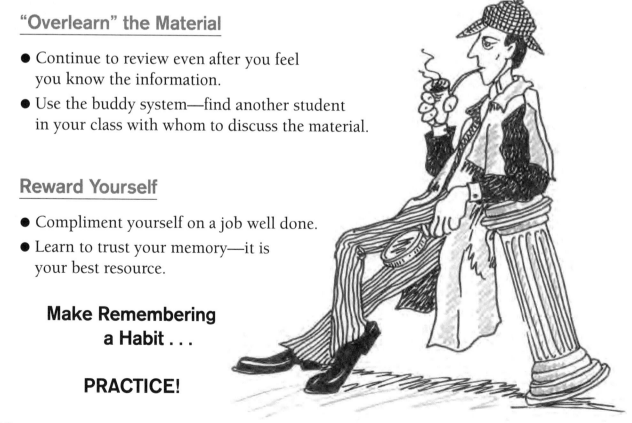

Mnemonic strategies are memory aids that provide a systematic approach for organizing and remembering facts that have no apparent link or connection of their own.

Why Use Mnemonics?

- Provides tools necessary to memorize and recall almost any information
- Provides steps to process material to avoid forgetting
- Provides pathways for these steps with fun and ease

Using Mnemonics

Apply all of your senses to the active process of learning and combine them whenever possible.

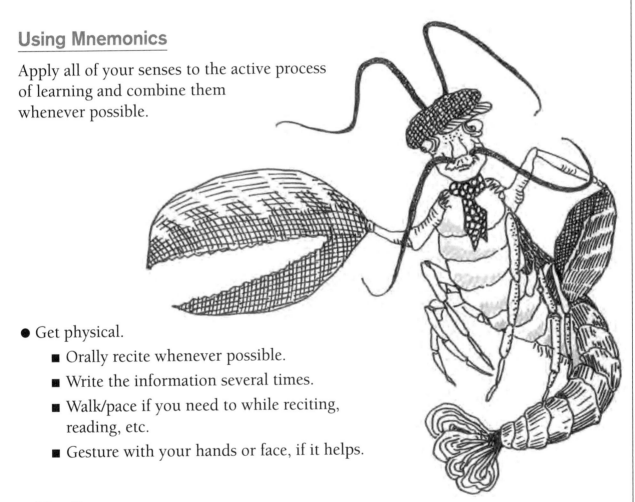

- Get physical.
  - Orally recite whenever possible.
  - Write the information several times.
  - Walk/pace if you need to while reciting, reading, etc.
  - Gesture with your hands or face, if it helps.

- Visualize.
  - Form clear pictures in your mind.
  - The mind remembers pictures more easily and for longer periods than it does words.
  - Picture yourself doing the activity

- Link new information to old information.

  - Ask yourself "What do I already know about about this?"

  - Group or "chunk" material together.

  - Remember similar/associated material when memory is blocked (serves to "jog" memory).

  - Link something physical to each idea. *Example:* link one item to each article of clothing you wear. Review out loud each time you get dressed. See *Study Time Warmup* on page 70.

MEMORY TIPS

- Match material to be learned with the most effective memory technique/mnemonic device.

- Combine memory techniques whenever possible (doubles the chances of long-term memory).

- Always repeat out loud as you write.

- Use 3" x 5" cards.

  - Write one entry per card.

  - Place card in upper left corner of mirror, bulletin board, locker, etc.

  - On tests, when your memory recall fails, write the alphabet in capital letters on the page and systematically review each letter in order to jog your memory. Ask yourself, "Does it begin with this letter?" If this does not work, try reviewing the alphabet backwards by looking at one letter at a time.

STRATEGY	DEFINITION	EXAMPLE
Mind Map	Organize mental maps from known information, then fill in missing information (details, main ideas, categories/parts, diagram labels)	government — president, congress, supreme court — Lincoln, Senate, House, Chase
Visual Chains	A visual cycle of pictures and/or words (cause/effect, linking systems, sequencing)	O_2 ... CO_2
Acronyms	Let the first letter of each word in a sentence represent the first letter of the words/list you wish to memorize (lists, sequencing)	**H**uron **O**ntario **M**ichigan **E**rie **S**uperior
Word Links	Use the meaning of one word to associate with another (definitions, pairs)	The capital of Oregon is Salem. (Think: There are many sailboats in Oregon because it's on the ocean. What do you do with these boats? "Sail 'em.")
Poems, Rhymes, Nonsense Verses, Lyrics	Using a familiar tune, substitute information to be learned (details, sequencing)	"Mary Had a Little Lamb" "The ABC Song" "In 1492, Columbus sailed the ocean blue."

STRATEGY	DEFINITION	EXAMPLE
Take-a-Trip	Visualize familiar objects around a room and attach some information/word with each object (lists)	dresser desk books bed
Acrostics	Make up a sentence using the first letter of each word (sequencing, lists)	**F**ine **D**oes **B**oy **G**ood **E**very (musical scale)
Picture Objects	Using a familiar object, associate information around it (lists, details)	Picture your finger. To learn prepositions, think of the action involved (around, to, from, etc.).
Hook-Ups	Using one word or series of letters, "hook up" information beginning with the same letter (details, categories/parts, lists)	**N** — New Mexico, North Carolina, Nevada **A** — Alabama, Alaska, Arkansas **T** — Texas, Tennessee
Make a Tape	Make a tape recording of information to be learned (vocabulary, spelling, lists, foreign languages, sequences, almost anything)	Play it repeatedly over several days. Play it just before sleeping at night.
Write It!	Write it repeatedly and say it aloud as you write (almost anything)	Write it just before you go to sleep.

STRATEGY	DEFINITION	EXAMPLE
Numbers	Write the numbers to be remembered (sequences)	Notice a special sequence and associate it with some familiar date. (birthday) 2　　17　　04 mo.　day　year
Poetry	The best way to remember poetry is to break it into small, meaningful sections (detail, sequencing)	Remember the story. Practice the meter/rhythm.
Sayings	Link information with a famous saying and substitute words (details)	A penny saved is . . . No pencil is as sharp as . . .
Mental Pictures	Visualize how you see or expect to see a total picture (diagrams)	Close your eyes and visualize an X-ray view of the skeleton from the head down.
Create an Experience	Mentally and visually create/recall an experience and link information to be learned with what you do (sequences, details)	Imagine yourself making cookies, building a bookshelf, etc., step-by-step. Plug information to be learned into each step.

1. **Clarify** – fully understand what it is you want to learn and memorize.

2. **Motivate** – intend to learn, remember, and concentrate on the new information; develop a strong, realistic purpose; clearly choose to remember.

3. **Categorize** – define the information to be learned and its intended purpose; choose between short- and long-term memory storage.

4. **Organize** – group information so that main ideas and details are connected; relate new information to known material.

5. **Plan** – select the best strategy/technique to fit the material and need.

6. **Review** – repeat the information, combining as many of the five senses as possible; make it a habit.

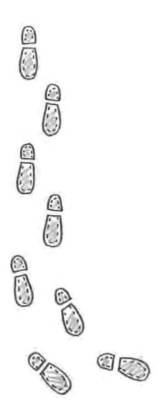

All languages have certain common aspects. No language is completely "foreign." You should apply many memory strategies to understand and remember what you read and hear. Learning to *think* in the language is the ultimate goal. This includes speaking and reading fluently and refraining from "translating words into English and then back again."

Learning a second language is not as difficult as it may seem if it is approached in a systematic, organized, and persistent manner. Use the following steps to achieve success! Remember to study aloud, review often, use flash cards (see *The Magic of Flash Cards* on page 112), and be an active—not passive—learner.

SET YOUR GOALS TO THINK IN THE FOREIGN LANGUAGE, THEN TRY TO:

- Read it and translate it into your own language.
- Understand the spoken language.
- Speak it.

KEEP UP WITH DAILY ASSIGNMENTS

REVIEW OVER AND OVER AGAIN

Identify Your Strengths and Weaknesses

(Write S for strength and W for weakness.)

____ reading the language

____ understanding the spoken language

____ composing thoughts in the language

____ keeping up with new vocabulary

____ translating

____ writing the language

Recognize Common Problems

LACKING AN UNDERSTANDING OF ENGLISH GRAMMAR

- Do not understand grammatical terms
- Do not understand idiom

FALLING BEHIND ON ASSIGNMENTS

- Vocabulary (memorization and spelling)
- Reading assignments
- Grammar study

Progressive Steps In Learning

MASTER ONE LEVEL, THEN MOVE ON TO THE NEXT ONE

- Learn the meanings of words (various forms/tenses)
- Learn simple phrases/sentences (idioms)
- Master word order (the relationships of words in clauses or sentences)
- Pronounce words or translate them in complex sentences
- Think "in the language"

Think of all of the senses you used as a child to learn your first language. Did you listen to those around you in order to learn vocabulary? Did you imitate their sounds by speaking? Did you decode the strange symbols in books in order to learn the meanings of printed words, phrases, and sentences? Did you try to recreate your own stories by writing?

Of course you did! So it is with any language. You can use these same methods successfully to learn a second language. By repeating these important steps, you can build your memory so that it will function in a foreign language. With practice and persistence, the language soon will cease to be "foreign!"

Listening

● Ask yourself this question: "How did I first learn English?" Understand that listening comes first.

● Intend to listen with the aim of repeating what you hear.

● Look up the pronunciation guide in your book.

● Listen for:
  ■ the sounds of words and how they flow together.
  ■ the meanings of words in phrases.

● Use any or all listening aids available.
  ■ Use listening labs at school.
  ■ Make your own tapes.
  ■ Check out tapes from the library/media center.
  ■ Go to foreign films.
  ■ Watch educational TV language courses.
  ■ Listen to foreign students talk.

Speaking

● Intend to speak the language and to use it as often as possible.

  ■ In the beginning, expect to be slow and to mispronounce words and use words incorrectly.

  ■ To form a good habit, immediately correct any mistakes.

● Emphasize recitation.

  ■ This is especially important.

  ■ Spend 80% of your time on this.

  ■ Practice, practice, practice!

● Learn grammar correctly.

  ■ Why learn grammar?

    ▲ It makes the language "second nature."

    ▲ It helps you to construct your own sentences.

    ▲ It helps you understand what others say and write.

● Helpful Hints

  ■ Know how to use and apply memorized lists of detached words.

  ■ Use dictionaries.

  ■ Attach some real meaning to your memorizing.

  ■ Whenever you don't understand a new grammatical term, ask the teacher or look up the term.

  ■ Be sure to memorize the exceptions to the rules and recite them in phrases and sentences.

Reading

- *Intend* to become proficient in understanding written material.

- Use the text.
    - Look for notes regarding reading assignments.
    - Be familiar with resources in the text such as the glossary or dictionary in the back of the book.

- Try to read the entire assignment the first time without translating it.
    - Use context clues.

- Try to rapidly progress from word-to-word translation to an understanding of complete phrases and sentences.

- Always reread a passage soon after translating it.

- Break unknown words into their elements and determine the meaning of the elements.
    - Learn root words, affixes, prefixes.

- Learn "cognate" words (words that have a common heritage).

- Read aloud when possible.
    - Hear yourself speak the language.
    - Work toward fluency and expression.

Writing

- *Intend* to learn to write the language correctly and easily.

- Write in phrases at first.
    - Write your thoughts as you think them.

- Pay attention to spelling, word order/form, and irregularities.

- Proofread your writing by reading it aloud.

TEST-TAKING SKILLS

FOCUS ON

*T*EST-TAKING *S*KILLS

1. Improve test grades by becoming "test-wise."

2. Recognize test anxiety and turn it into positive energy.

3. Plan ahead to make appropriate study time for tests.

4. Form a study group.

5. Compile and edit class/text notes and handouts into useful study sheets.

6. Always ask the teacher about the test format a few days before the test.

7. Become familiar with intelligent guessing strategies.

8. Review specifics on how to take each type of test.

9. Know how to use your time wisely during the test.

10. Know essay direction words and how to interpret them.

11. Remember the results of your learning styles assessment.

12. Choose test-taking tools that focus on your strengths and minimize your weaknesses.

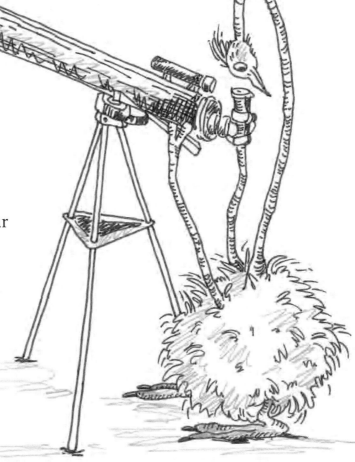

In order to do well on a test, you must know the subject matter as well as how to take the test. Knowing how to demonstrate your full potential and the knowledge that you have learned is called "test-wiseness." Your intelligence and previous knowledge combined with new information that you learn in preparation for tests should result in your ability to perform well and succeed.

The following pages will give you numerous strategies to apply before, during, and after taking a test. Research indicates that as many as twenty points can be gained simply by using good "test-wiseness" tools.

Using your study time effectively to prepare for a test is a key factor in taking tests. Your approach to studying will be determined by the type of test. Basically, there are two types of exams:
(1) objective (multiple-choice, true/false, matching, fill-in-the-blank) and
(2) subjective (essay). Both of these "types" can be found in standardized as well as non-standardized exams.

Standardized tests are those that have established norms (the average achievement of a large group) which allow teachers to compare your score against the scores of other students. These tests often are given in booklet form to large groups and are used to predict your achievement and skills in certain areas.

Some examples of standardized tests are:

1. **Achievement Tests**—cover many subjects; measure your knowledge level in the specific area

2. **Aptitude Tests**—predict your success in a course or program; often determine entrance and placement by colleges, SAT tests

3. **Diagnostic Tests**—show strengths and weaknesses in a specific subject area; often determine placement of level in a particular subject

Non-standardized tests do not have norms and usually are the tests most teachers give to "gauge" a student's knowledge. Such tests usually are constructed by the teacher and are taken by the student. The remainder of this chapter will deal with non-standardized tests and how to prepare for them and take them with success.

There are many important and critical aspects that lead to good test scores. Probably the most important are an intention to do well on the test and to have a positive mental attitude before the test. Believing that you are capable of achieving the score you want is half the battle.

If you can understand that testing is an essential part of the learning process and that you actually can learn from tests, you are that much ahead of the game. This also can aid in learning how to control test anxiety and change negative energy into positive energy. Recognizing that tests do not always measure what you learn and that some teachers make poor tests should help you to be kinder to yourself when results are lower than you anticipate. If you rely on thorough knowledge of the subject matter, common sense, and learned test-taking skills, you can relax and expect success when taking a test!

Studying, understanding, and applying the following information about how to become "test-wise" could possibly raise your test scores for years to come. It definitely will make you a more relaxed and successful student! As you review these test-taking techniques, focus on the elements that best fit your learning modality: visual, auditory, or kinesthetic.

A few suggested test-taking aids for the three modalities are:

VISUAL:	AUDITORY:	KINESTHETIC:
• Use "cue" words • Use graphic organizers • Form pictures in your mind	• Talk to yourself to reduce stress • Repeat mnemonics to yourself • Read all directions twice to yourself	• Relax muscles in body • Stretch in your chair • Breathe slowly

- absent from school and didn't make up the work
- didn't pay attention (listen) in class
- didn't do homework
- didn't care
- didn't read text
- waited too long to begin studying
- wasn't organized
- didn't get enough sleep
- studied wrong material
- changed too many answers
- poor attitude about the subject
- didn't review from day-to-day
- cramming was ineffective
- didn't budget time to study
- overconfident
- test anxiety
- memory block during testing
- think the teacher is unfair
- don't like the teacher
- lack of test-wiseness
- ran out of time
- didn't check answers
- left too many answers blank

Ways to Avoid Poor Performance

1. Keep up with your studies.
2. Learn good study habits and apply them.
3. Train your memory.
4. Become test-wise.
5. Be positive.
6. Be organized.

Grades, grades, grades! A test grade reflects how well you did on one particular test—it doesn't necessarily measure your intelligence, how much you learned, your creativity, or your worth as a person. It's important to keep this in mind and to view test grades in proper perspective with the rest of your life.

If you have "butterflies" in your stomach before a test, don't be disturbed. Most people get them. A little extra "charge" or adrenaline can help you perform at your best. Turning that extra bit of energy into a positive attribute actually can increase your test score. However, real test anxiety can block your memory and prevent you from doing well. By understanding and accepting test anxiety—then applying successful tools to conquer it—you can overcome this barrier and practice effective test-taking strategies.

Carefully consider the test anxiety information on pages 208–210 and try some of the suggestions the next time you find yourself becoming anxious before, during, or after a test.

- nervousness

- fear of . . .

    . . . forgetting

    . . . the unknown

    . . . not finishing the test

    . . . not studying

    the right material

- non-stop talking

- withdrawal

- fidgeting

- dread

- self "put-down"

- lack of concentration

- change in appetite

- high degree of confusion

- nausea

- sweaty palms

- sleeplessness

- nosebleeds

- memory blocks

- increased and noticeable worry

- deep concern about a personal reflection on you

- extreme quietness

- inappropriate laughter

- extreme lack of patience

- anger

- boasting

- inadequate preparation

1. Stop Yourself

When you first have any negative thought, immediately begin positive "self-talk." This is the way in which you communicate with yourself "inside your head." Interrupt the continuous thoughts of worry by giving yourself permission to be concerned as you channel your energy into doing something to help yourself. Once you have admitted that you are anxious, accept it and continue trying to improve the situation. This focuses your attention on a positive action rather than on negative worry.

2. Plan Your Attack

Use some of these strategies as alternatives to non-productive anxiety and worry. Be sure to try each strategy. You have everything to gain. Once you find several strategies that work for you, you can rely on them with great trust. Just knowing that you are in control of the situation (and can handle your feelings) will allow you to perform much better during the test. Practice these at your desk or at home often. You will need these to break your anxiety during a test, so using them at home in the "study" environment will help you to recall them better.

Visualize   about somewhere you really enjoy being—the seashore, the mountains, etc. Literally close your eyes and put yourself there.

Daydream   about something you especially enjoy—a hobby, sport, vacation, certain location or time, someone special, etc. Make it a vivid dream with warm, comfortable surroundings. Or, try thinking about nothing and letting your mind wander.

Make Up   a story about anything preposterous. Blow it "up and out of reality"—exaggerate! Imagine the worst thing that could happen to you if you did poorly on the test. Make it funny and very unrealistic. Soon you will be laughing at yourself.

Recall   the helpful tools and methods you have learned and have come to trust. They will aid your memory. There are so many—and you can count on them whenever you want or need them.

Breathe   by taking several slow, controlled, deep breaths. Concentrate on the movement of the air as it goes in and out of your body. Focus all of your attention on breathing!

Notice   your body posture and any tense muscles. Make a conscious effort to relax those muscles. First, tense each muscle as much as possible for a few seconds and then relax it. Tell yourself that you are now relaxed. You may want to "relax" only those muscles that you can feel. Or, begin at the top of your body and work down to your toes. Focus your entire attention toward this effort. Try to use a relaxed posture while taking the test. Do not hunch over the desk, raise your shoulders, or put your head way down.

Do Something   physical, such as exercise (if the situation permits it). Roll your head, neck, and shoulders, or stretch frequently.

HAVE SELF-CONFIDENCE!

In School

- Study the teacher for clues to what's important.
  - Voice (volume, inflection, speed changes)
  - Gestures (face, hand, body)
  - Materials (handouts, models, films, overhead transparencies)
  - Repetition of main ideas/details
  - Know the type(s) of questions the teacher may ask (requests for details, general overview of the subject matter, objective or subjective tests, time sequencing, graphic information such as charts, graphs, maps, etc.).

- In Class...
  - Intend to learn.
  - Listen carefully.
  - Take good notes and review them often.
  - Ask good questions, including what material is to be covered on the test and what form the test will take (T/F, multiple-choice, essay, etc.).
  - Try to condense and capture important ideas into a mind map or outline at the end of each class.
  - Complete the *Test Review Sheet* on page 214. The more you know about the test, the better you can prepare for it.

- Get information from other students.
  - Talk with others who have previously taken the class.
  - Get old tests.
    - ▲ Don't expect the exact same questions on the next test.
    - ▲ Look at the general concepts covered.
    - ▲ Look at the format (T/F, matching, multiple-choice, short answer, essay, etc.).
    - ▲ Watch for the amount of questions taken from class lectures, reading assignments, handouts, audio-visual aids, and other assignments.
    - ▲ Look for trick questions.
    - ▲ Watch for the information that wasn't covered.

    - ▲ Did the test require recall of facts or reasoning skills?

At Home

- Refer to the note-taking strategies related to creating study sheets and the reading strategies in other chapters of this book.

- A few days before the test, list concepts you think are most important and ask the teacher (at a convenient time) if these are appropriate topics to study for the test.
  - Choose a time when the teacher has set aside a few moments to spend with individual students (after class, before school, or after school are good).
  - This demonstrates to the teacher that you have taken the interest and initiative in studying for the test.
  - What have you got to lose? Most teachers will be very helpful and will be delighted that you have an interest in the class.

- Gather all of the study materials you will need.

- Review any class/reading notes, handouts, study sheets, 3" x 5" cards, texts, course outlines, out-of-class assignments, old tests, graphic organizers, etc.
  - Pay particular attention to:
    - ▲ Lists
    - ▲ Italicized or boldface words or phrases
    - ▲ Material "weighted" in class (concepts stressed by the teacher through repetition or amount of time given to a concept)

- Divide material into what you know well, what you need to review, what is unfamiliar, etc.
  - Color code or label this material. For example:
    - ▲ A or green = material I know well
    - ▲ B or yellow = material I need to review
    - ▲ C or red = material that is unfamiliar

- Construct additional 3" x 5" cards. See *The Magic of Flash Cards* on page 112. which include:
  - Vocabulary
  - Definitions
  - Formulas
  - Lists of causes/effects, pros/cons
  - Summaries of concepts (cue words and phrases)
    (Note: These are especially good for open-book tests!)

- Make graphic organizers as review study guides. See *Creating a Graphic Organizer* on page 119.

- Turn chapter headings (and sub-headings within chapters) into possible test questions.

- Make up questions about material in the text and your notes. Then answer the questions under time pressure.

- Review specific note-taking techniques and rehearse your "plan of attack" (especially important for essay tests).

- Form a "study group."

- Have someone quiz you over the materials using the same format as the test.

- Quickly review the material just before going to sleep. Your subconscious will continue to "rehearse" the information.

- Get a full night's sleep before the test.

- Have the positive attitude that <u>you've studied</u> and <u>will do well on the test</u>.

BE ORGANIZED!

*T*EST REVIEW SHEET

Class _____ Teacher _____ Name _____

Period _____ Study Partner(s): _____

TEST INFORMATION

Test Date: _____ Test Time: _____ % of Grade: _____ Total Points: _____

TYPE	# OF QUESTIONS	POINT VALUE	TOTAL VALUE	TYPES:
_____				true/false
_____				multiple choice
_____				matching
_____				fill-in-the-blank
_____				essay
_____				open book
_____				take home

CONTENT

1. Main Concepts: _____   Notes: _____

_____   _____

_____   _____

_____   _____

_____   _____

_____   _____

2. Textbook Chapters: _____

_____

3. Other Books: _____

_____

4. Handouts: _____

_____

5. Previous Tests: _____

_____

6. Lab Reports: _____

_____

7. Vocabulary Words:

_____ _____ _____

_____ _____ _____

_____ _____ _____

8. Notes: _____

_____

_____

Why Form a Study Group?

- Reinforces what you already know
- Provides the opportunity to practice and review
- Allows you to meet other students and enjoy constructive studying in a fun atmosphere
- Enables you to learn new information from others
- Promotes a better understanding of confusing or unknown concepts
- Allows for better coverage of the material
- Helps you to be more likely to study if others are counting on you
- Adds to your learning. It does not replace reading and studying all the material yourself before you attend the first study group meeting

How to Form a Successful Study Group

STEP 1 ☞ Identify 1–5 students in your class that closely match your expectations in grades, ability, and motivation.

- Do not include anyone who will not "pull their own weight" and be an active, equally contributing member.
- Do not include anyone who is unreliable.

STEP 2 ☞ Contact the students to arrange a meeting time and place. (Plan only one to start and be sure to get all necessary phone numbers/email addresses.)

STEP 3 ☞ Before the first meeting, have each student choose an area to "specialize" in, covering a specific portion of the material in detail combining text/class notes, handouts, lab reports, etc.

- Every student volunteers to cover the same amount of material Example: 2 text chapters, 2 major topics, etc.

- Each student constructs study sheets/graphic organizers of their special area to cover and makes copies for everyone to be distributed at the first meeting.
  - Combine all class/text notes, handout information, lab reports, etc. into study sheets/graphics for that specific topic.
  - Decide if everyone will pay for their own copy costs or contribute to one account to cover all copy costs before the first meeting.

STEP 4 ☞ At the first meeting:

- Exchange names, phone numbers, email addresses again.
- Set specific goals for the group with reasonable time lines for that meeting.
- Appoint one member to be the "task master."
  - Keeps everyone focused on the topic at hand
  - Rotate members each meeting to be the new "task master"

- Discuss/brainstorm:
  - The instructor's teaching style
  - The overview of the subject matter (skim through text, class notes)
  - Any in-class test review notes
  - Possible format of test
  - Any obvious possible essay questions
  - Any information gathered from former students, texts, etc.
  - All possible sources for information (don't forget handouts, class discussion notes, presentation notes, etc.)

STEP 5 ☞ Each member:

- Presents/teaches material they "specialized" in.
- Distributes and reviews their study sheets/graphic organizers for the material they "specialized" in covering.
- Quizzes other group members on material covered.

STEP 6 ☞ All group members:

- Discuss and question all topics and materials.
- Make any necessary additions/corrections to study sheets/ graphic organizers.
- Discuss test format and possible questions.

STEP 7 ☞ Test each other for "weak spots" covering all the material to be tested.

STEP 8 ☞ Make a "plan of action" for getting additional help if needed.

STEP 9 ☞ Plan a second session, if necessary (and if the first one was successful).

- Make sure every member has a clear set of goals for the next meeting.
- Be certain that each member understands his or her particular assignment.
- Be sure everyone volunteers to be a specialist for equal amounts of information and signs up specific chapters, main topics, etc.
- Honestly and tactfully discuss any problems that occurred during the first session and brainstorm solutions.
- Designate a time and place for the next session and get a commitment to attend from each member.

Additional Suggestions for Forming a Successful Study Group

- The library is a poor place to meet. It will stifle creative excitement because of the noise restrictions.

- Secure any necessary permission ahead of time for the meeting time and place. Parents are usually more than willing to supply snacks for a good study group meeting but do not like surprises.

- Use the structured study block system (see *Rules for Study Time: The Backbone of Success* on page 65) to maintain focus and effectively use your time.

- Food and beverages add fun and excitement. Remember to reserve them for breaks between study blocks.

- Allow enough time to accomplish your goals so you do not feel rushed but not enough time to foster a gab session.

- Don't forget to appoint a new member as a "task master" each meeting.

- If holding more than one session, take turns in keeping any necessary records, lists, etc.

- Understand that everyone pays equally for copy costs, etc. that might occur due to an exchange of notes, study sheets, etc.

In-Class Tests

- Mechanical pencil, extra lead
- Erasable pens that work
- Good erasers
- Compass, protractor, straightedge, ruler
- Calculator
- Correction fluid

Hint: *If you need extra blank paper during a test to recreate your graphic organizers, use as scratch paper for calculations or for any reason, never take one from your backpack, binder, etc., or borrow one from another student. Ask your teacher for blank paper and have him/her sign it before taking it back to your seat. This will save you time and embarrassment should there be any questions about your use of a blank sheet.*

Memorized graphic organizers are extremely helpful and will greatly reduce your stress as you use them throughout the test. See Creating A Graphic Organizer on page 119.

OPEN-BOOK TESTS IN CLASS

Be sure to "clear" with the teacher all supplies and references you intend to bring into the classroom for the open-book test.

- All of the items listed for in-class tests
- Textbooks, binders, dictionary, thesaurus, writing guide, atlas, almanac, quick academic guides
  - Use "flags" or small Post-it® Notes to place on page edges to signal or group main ides, topics, and details. Place them all around the book edges in different locations so when the book is closed you can see all of them.
  - Color code flags according to topic.
  - Place one large Post-it® Note on the front of the text as an index to your color coding system for that book. Don't trust your mind to remember this because you can become confused in the middle of a test.
- All class/text notes, handouts, study sheets, and/or graphic organizers

- Flash cards, in appropriate order, on split rings
  - Clearly label each set of flash cards by using the top card to list the main topic (sub-topics, details/examples if needed) if using more than one set.

Hint: *Time is precious, as these tests usually have more questions than closed-book tests. You will most likely run out of time if you depend on finding the answers you need just by having the text and your notes available. You must study for this test just as you would for a closed-book test, and you must organize all your materials.*

Highly organized materials are vital for saving time during open-book tests. Use color coding and lines to section off information on 3" x 5" cards, place labeled flags on page edges of graphic organizers, charts/graphs, lists, and any specific material for easy and immediate access. You should be able to locate information in 10 seconds!

Take-Home Tests

- All of the items listed for In-Class Tests
- Go to the library to research and read the latest information on your topic in magazine articles, scientific publications, etc.
- Use old tests
- Do some networking:
  - Phone, email, or personally contact community resources (look in the phone book)
  - Contact friends, parents and their friends, students previously in this class
  - Get together in a study group (see *Forming a Study Group* on page 215)
  - Use the Internet

Hint: *Essays need to be very well written. Have several people proofread your essays for consistency, appropriate content, clarity, structure, grammar, and punctuation. Use a student handbook as a guide (see Essay Tests on page 240 and Organize Your Materials! on page 41 for a great reference book). Use a typed format rather than handwritten if possible. Reread the question several times and make sure you answer it directly.*

Double-check all objective test answers for silly errors (transposing a math problem answer to the incorrect space, or not labeling the solution correctly). Make sure all your writing is legible. Also, thoroughly check all calculations, reference sources, etc.

Watch for these "qualifying" words in test questions. They can be a real help or hindrance to your answers!

General (usually true)	**Specific (always true)**		
seldom	always	nobody	including
generally	all	no one	many
probably	never	because	few
most	none	only	equal to
often	frequently	must	inequality
some	more than	weak	equality
sometimes	less than	everyone	superior
usually	neither	true	inferior
	both	false	whole
	everybody	negative	part
	impossible	positive	specifically
	absolutely	except	strong

Whenever you read one of these words in test directions, questions or answers . . .

- circle the word to fix your attention on that word

- consider the question/answer very carefully

INTELLIGENT GUESSING STRATEGIES

The intelligent guessing strategies on pages 222–226 should be used only as a last resort if you don't know the answer and if you will be penalized for guessing. If the test scoring system does not deduct points for wrong answers, it is always better to guess than to leave questions unanswered. Be sure to find out if guessing is penalized before taking the test.

Always choose an answer or "fill in" the answer and flag it (circle the number, draw a star or question mark beside the question, etc.) so you can quickly determine the questions that need special attention when you are checking/reviewing your test. Fill in the answer the first time instead of "skipping" it with the intention of returning. It is very possible that time might run out and you won't have the opportunity to return to the question. Use any extra time to double-check flagged questions. Think carefully before changing your first answer. Odds are that your first response is the correct one.

Research indicates that appropriate and correct application of intelligent guessing techniques can raise test scores significantly. Learn the following strategies well and use them with care. Remember to apply them only as a last resort if your recall fails or if you are totally unfamiliar with the material.

 ©Incentive Publications, Inc., Nashville, TN

Statements/Words Most Likely to Be True	Statements/Words Most Likely to Be False	Type of Test	Examples
The most "general" statement		multiple-choice true/false	The poem *The Cemetery of Whales* by Yevgeny Yevtuschenko: a. is not translatable b. is basically a criticism of communism c. refers only to situations in Russia d. appeals only to Jewish people
	absolute statements	multiple-choice	It is always hot in August. Words that are absolute: all — no one always — only everybody — must impossible — never absolutely — none nobody — everyone
	unfamiliar/unknown words and phrases	multiple-choice true/false	Any words that you don't recall seeing during your study time.
	humorous alternatives, insults, jokes	multiple-choice matching (if there are extras)	

Statements/Words Most Likely to Be True	Statements/Words Most Likely to Be False	Type of Test	Examples
The most complete statements		multiple-choice	When memorizing information: a. start the night before b. have a positive attitude and intend to remember c. gather all the information together d. cram
	If alternatives range in value, eliminate the two extremes	multiple-choice	The population of Boulder is: a. 250,000 b. 85,000 c. 43,500 d. 10,000
"All of the above" choice		multiple-choice	When constructing study sheets for a test, include: a. reading notes b. class notes c. graphs d. all of the above
	Statements that contain reasons or qualifying answers	true/false multiple-choice	Paul did poorly on the test because he went to a movie the night before instead of studying. F because, except, not

  ©Incentive Publications, Inc., Nashville, TN

Statements/Words Most Likely to Be True	Statements/Words Most Likely to Be False	Type of Test	Examples
The longest choice		multiple-choice	The Great Gatsby: a. exploits infidelity <u>b.</u> demonstrates the revenge of the downtrodden on the rich c. occurs in Minneapolis d. illustrates Southern hospitality
If two choices are opposite, choose one of them		multiple-choice	Sigmund Freud: <u>a.</u> developed the theory of psychoanalysis b. did not develop the theory of psychoanalysis c. always advised the psychoanalysis for his patients d. felt that therapy should be carried out in a sanitarium
"All of the above" choice	If two choices are nearly the same, choose neither one.	multiple-choice	The most important thing that Abraham Lincoln did politically was to: a. wield an axe b. split rails <u>c.</u> issue the Emancipation Proclamation d. be shot in the Ford Theatre after the war

Statements/Words Most Likely To Be True	Statements/Words Most Likely To Be False	Type of Test	Examples
Answer in the middle, especially with the most words		multiple-choice	When you don't know the right answer, you should: a. leave it blank b. answer using test-wise strategies and then flag it c. go to the next one

A Closer Look at Negatives

Negatives are words or prefixes that change the meaning to the opposite.

Common Negative Words	Common Negative Prefixes	
not	un	non
except	in	im
false	il	ir
	dis	

- Be especially alert to negatives in objective test questions.

- Sometimes it is helpful to circle the negative words and prefixes in questions and answers.

Double Negatives are statements which contain two negatives—usually one word and one prefix. Cross out both. Then, reread and answer.

Ex: He is ~~not un~~athletic.

Triple Negatives are statements which contain three negatives—usually one word and two prefixes. Cross out two of the negatives. Then, reread and answer.

Ex: It is ~~not un~~kind to be impatient.

Things You Should Know About Cramming

- Use it as a last resort.
- Your recall of information is limited to one to two days.
- Your learning and the amount of material you can cover are limited due to lack of time.
- The general scope and understanding of the subject is limited.
- It takes longer to learn information under pressure.

How To Cram If You Must

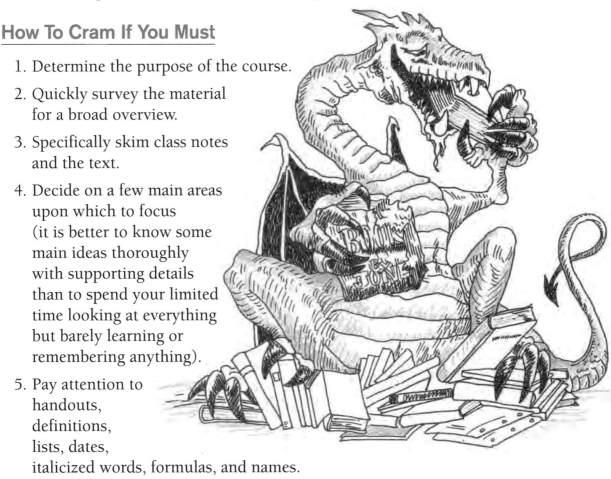

1. Determine the purpose of the course.

2. Quickly survey the material for a broad overview.

3. Specifically skim class notes and the text.

4. Decide on a few main areas upon which to focus (it is better to know some main ideas thoroughly with supporting details than to spend your limited time looking at everything but barely learning or remembering anything).

5. Pay attention to handouts, definitions, lists, dates, italicized words, formulas, and names.

6. Make study sheets, mind maps, graphic organizers, flash cards, etc.

7. Review, recite, and memorize using mnemonic devices whenever possible.

8. Review strategies on how to take each type of test. (See pages 232–252.)

9. Go into the test with the attitude that you will do well with what you were able to study.

10. Don't waste time on the questions you don't know—skip them.

11. Review and apply the "intelligent guessing strategies" when possible.

- Arrive early enough to:
  - Gather all needed materials
  - Choose a quiet part of the room (a corner in the front of the room is best)
    - ▲ to avoid the distractions of those in front of you
    - ▲ to hear any oral directions clearly
    - ▲ to read the chalkboard better

- "Settle in" and get comfortable.
  - Visit the restroom.
  - Clean your glasses (if you have any).
  - Get a drink of water.
  - Remove all distracting items from your desk.
  - Sit erect in the chair to stay alert.
  - Relax (breathe deeply, stretch, etc.).

- Quickly glance through your study sheets for a last review, if you feel like it.

- Don't talk to others about test material—it is too confusing!

- If you know you are unfamiliar with the test room and feel uncomfortable about taking the test there, it is a good idea to make a brief visit to the test room before the test date to become comfortable with the environment.

- Bring all of your previous experiences and learning with you. Trust your study skills and test-taking strategies!

FOCUS ON CONCENTRATING AND HAVE A POSITIVE ATTITUDE!

Use Your Time Wisely

1. Put your name on all pages of the test.

2. Think only positive thoughts.

3. Make a conscious effort to relax your neck, shoulders, and upper back.

4. Write down key words and phrases from any oral directions.

5. Don't start writing immediately. Look over the entire test to learn the number and kind of questions.

6. Budget your time. Allow yourself time after you have finished the test to double-check your answers.

7. Read all directions twice. Circle key words and be careful not to read more into questions than is actually there.

8. Recreate graphic organizers or outlines you've memorized on any blank spaces available on the test. If no space is available, ask the teacher for a blank piece of paper and have her sign or initial it at the top. This will remind her that it was a blank sheet and that she gave it to you. *Never get your own paper from under your seat/desk, binder, or backpack.*

9. Deliberately ignore the pace of classmates and proceed with a steady pace.

10. Answer all questions. Use intelligent guessing strategies for those you don't know—flag those questions and come back to them to double-check your answers. (Be sure to find out if there is a penalty for guessing.)

11. Never change an answer unless it is clearly wrong.

12. Your subconscious will continue to "work" on questions about which you are unsure. Sometimes a question/answer will trigger recall for another question/answer.

13. If you get "stuck" . . .

- Reread the question and break it down into small units.

- Search for the "cue" or "clue" words and define them mentally.

- Carefully reread the answer choices (read the stem—the "question" above the answers—first, and then each answer with it).

- Put yourself in your teacher's position and try to determine what he or she wants.

- Try to recall particular phrases the teacher might have repeated/related to the idea/concept.

- Visualize the event, time line, section of the book, etc., in which the answer might be found.

- Brainstorm associated concepts and try to recall similar information.

- Put the question into your own words for better understanding, being very careful not to change the meaning.

- Draw a picture or diagram to really "see" it.

- Write synonyms in margins to help you jog your memory for specific words.

- Write the alphabet at the top of the page and quickly review each letter forward (or backward).

14. Check your answers.

- Are they readable?

- Do they answer the questions asked?

- Are they in the correct answer spaces?

- Have they been transposed correctly from "workspace?"

- Have they been well-written (if an essay) to include an introduction, specific and well-supported facts, and a conclusion?

Multiple-Choice Test Strategies

- Know that they are the type most often given by teachers.
- Know that multiple-choice tests are designeed to test how well you recognize related information.
- Understand the directions.
  - Read all directions twice.
  - Is there one (or more than one) correct answer per question?
- Work quickly.
- "Flag" questions about which you are unsure, and continue.
- Answer all questions (never leave a blank unless you are not penalized for unanswered questions).

STEP 1:  Cover all answers with your hands to better focus on the stem (the "question" above the choices).

STEP 2: ☞ Study the stem and circle any qualifiers or key words (refer to *List of "Qualifiers"* on page 221).

STEP 3: ☞ Recall the answer before reading the choices.

STEP 4: ☞ Uncover the answers, then choose the answer that best matches yours.

STEP 5: ☞ Separate the questions or answers into smaller parts if you find them complicated or confusing.

STEP 6: ☞ Read all of the choices before making a decision.

STEP 7: ☞ Eliminate obviously wrong answers.

- Refer to *Intelligent Guessing Strategies* on page 222.
- Look for "clue" words or numbers.
- Watch for grammatical clues.
    - Noun/verb agreement between stem and answer
    - A/an in stem—answer begins with vowel
    - Plurals
- Be on the lookout for familiar phrases from lectures or the text.
- Immediately cross off "NONE OF THE ABOVE" or "ALL OF THE ABOVE" answer choices when you read through the answers and find one that makes either of these two incorrect.

STEP 8: ☞ When you get stuck, try reading the stem with each possible answer (separately).

STEP 9: ☞ If time permits, recheck your answers.

- Look for flagged questions first.
- Before changing any answers, be sure you have a very good reason to do so—your first response is usually correct.

True/False Test Strategies

- Realize that true/false tests are the most difficult to take.

- Know that true/false tests are measuring whether you can recognize specific facts and details.

- Understand the directions.
  - Read all of the directions twice.
  - Look to see if there is a given number of true or false statements.

Hint: *There usually are more true answers than false answers because they are easier to write. If you must guess, answer true because the odds are better.*

- Read carefully.
  - Do not analyze each question for deeper meaning.
  - If the question is confusing, break it in half and make sure you thoroughly understand each part.
  - Look at the question from the test maker's point of view.

- Watch for "qualifying" words:

– because	– all	– all wrong/right
– no one	– never	– always
– nobody	– generally	– none
– only	– some	

(Refer to *List of "Qualifiers"* for more words on page 221.)

- Always answer the question.
  - Answer the questions, even if you are unsure. Then, flag the question for a quick review when checking over the test.
  - You may not have time to come back to the question—any answer is better than nothing (if there is no penalty for guessing).

- Find out before the test if there is a penalty for guessing or leaving the answer blank.

- Statements with "reasons" tend to be false (because they are incorrect or incomplete reasons).

- Don't change your answers.
  - Research shows that first answers usually are correct.
  - Be absolutely sure before changing an answer.

- Assume that the statement is true unless you determine it to be false.
  - It's easier to write true statements than to make false statements seem true.
  - All parts of a true/false question must be true before it can be true.
  - Cover the statement using two fingers. Reveal only one word at a time by moving your finger across the statement. Ask yourself with each word: "Does this word make it false?"

- Cross out all pairs of negatives, then reread the question.

MATCHING TESTS

Matching Test Strategies

- Matching tests are designed to measure how well you recognize specific facts and details

- Understand the directions well.
  - Find out if each answer is used once or more than once.

Hint: *The following matching system is highly successful, saves you time, and lowers frustration and stress by getting the right answer the first time and not having to change answers numerous times. It will load your brain with all the information before you begin to match items, sort out answers that are alike, and r emember where the cor rect answer is located within the column. Learn to work with how your brain works and not against it.*

- Read the longest column with the most words first (usually the right column with letters) and complete the following steps as you read:

STEP 1 ☞ Mark "like" answers.
Example: when you read down to "E" and remember it is a possible alternative to an answer you already read, "B", immediately write an "E" in front of the "B" so you will consider both answers when making the best choice for the match with the other column.

STEP 2 ☞ Cross off obviously wrong answers immediately.

STEP 3 ☞ Draw a horizontal line to mark the half-way point in this list. Since your brain has a strong memory for placement, you will recall if the correct answer is above the line or below the line when you start matching the two columns together.
Example: If the list consists of answers labeled A to Z, the line would be after the letter M

STEP 4 ☞ Now read the other (shorter, fewer words) column.

STEP 5 ☞ Begin matching the items.
- Cross off answers once they are used.
- Be sure to print your answers clearly and correctly.
- If you're stumped:
  - Close your eyes and try to picture the text page, text/class notes, study sheets, graphic organizers, or flash cards that contain the information you need.

Fill-In-The-Blank Test Strategies

- This type of test requires you to provide specific facts and details.
- On this type of test it is important to understand the directions well.
- Note if the response options are listed on another page or at the bottom of the questions page.
- Read the question carefully and look for clue words (especially just before the blanks).
  - a, an, the, these, those, they
  - Clue words indicate vowel/consonant, singular/plural words.
  - Singular verbs end in "s" most often before the blank. A verb that ends in "s" likely signals a singular noun.
  - Often they appear after the blank.
- Answer the question.
  - Write/print clearly.
  - Be sure your answer "fits" the question.
  - Sometimes the teacher uses sentences taken from the text.
- When you're stuck:
  - Brainstorm for a moment.
  - If you can't think of the exact word, write a synonym or definition for that word or phrase. Partial credit is better than none.
  - Write all possible answers. Flag the question and come back to it. Your mind will continue to think and possibly will recall the answer later.
  - Try to picture the concept at a certain place in your notes and/or text. Associate this with the concept.
  - Write the alphabet using one capital letter at a time to jog your memory for what the word might begin with, then go backwards if that does not work.
  - Draw a picture and silently talk yourself through it.

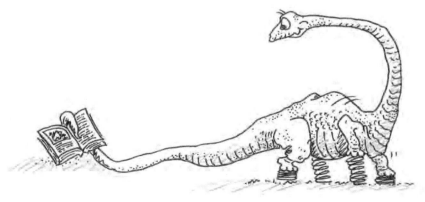

Number Test Strategies

● Number tests require that you provide reasons, proof, and specific answers.

● Understand the directions well. (They will usually ask you to cite rules or formulas and to apply these in order to arrive at a specific answer.)

● Write clearly.
   ■ Be sure each number is recognizable.
   ■ Keep numbers in proper columns or the spaces provided.

● Copy the problem correctly.
   ■ Make sure you have copied the problem correctly before working it.
   ■ Have in mind the correct answer label if one is required.
   ■ If answer columns are used, double-check the answer as you transfer it from the workspace to the correct answer column.

● Estimate the answer first.
   ■ Get a "ballpark" answer in mind.
   ■ For multiple-choice questions, work the problem before looking at the answers.

- Watch for measurement units.
  - Be sure to convert properly if necessary.
  - Label your answer correctly and double-check accuracy and legibility.

- Watch for "deadwood" numbers. Cross out obviously unnecessary facts or figures numbers that have been thrown in to cause confusion.

- Check the arithmetic of all problems.
  - Check even the simplest addition and subtraction steps.
  - Most wrong answers are due to simple mathematical errors.

- When you get stuck:
  - Watch for clue words such as additional, equally, less, etc.
  - Illustrate the problem by drawing a picture, diagram, or graph.
  - Reread the question by breaking it down into simple parts.
  - Change complicated and complex numbers into whole numbers and try to work the problem as an example.
  - Make an educated guess when all else fails (if you will not be penalized for guessing).
    - Eliminate unusual fractions and measurements.
    - Eliminate the highest and lowest answers in multiple-choice questions.

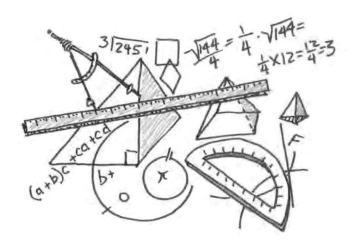

Essay Test Strategies

- Prepare before the test.

- Anticipate test questions.
  - Color code class and text notes if possible.
  - Make note of how much time the instructor devoted to each concept. The longer the time emphasis, the more probability there will be a question or two about this concept on the test.
  - Be sure to study definitions and lists.
  - Pay attention to handouts, study guides, and review materials from the teacher.

- Map out answers.
  - For each question that you think will be on the test:
    - ▲ Construct a brief outline (see *Essay Answer Format* on page 248).
    - ▲ Make a graphic organizer/mind map (see *Creating a Graphic Organizer* on page 119).
  - Be sure to include all main ideas and supporting details.

- Provide details and examples.
  - Key words/phrases (check spelling)
  - Accurate dates, names, facts, etc.
  - Relationships/connections with other concepts stressed in class

- Memorize your graphic organizer.
  - Practice reproducing it from memory so that you can reproduce it accurately and quickly on the test or blank paper at the beginning of the test.

- Make sure you have the three main ingredients of a successful essay:
  - Knowledge of the subject
  - Organization of ideas
  - Writing skills

● Find out in advance who is grading the essays and promote ideas that appeal to the grader.

● During the test, always listen carefully to all directions given by the teacher before beginning.

STEP 1: ☞ Read any general/specific directions the essay section provides. Do you have a choice of questions to answer or must all questions be answered?

STEP 2: ☞ Read all of the questions before you begin.

- Note how many points each essay question is worth and start with the one that is worth the most points.

- Jot down a few phrases about each question as you read through the test.

- This helps when you want to begin writing or choose the one you want to answer (if applicable).

- It jogs your memory.

- Reading all of the questions will keep you from repeating information.

STEP 3: ☞ Decide on a time limit for each question.

- Divide your time among the questions accordingly.

- Go to the next question if your time runs out.

- Four partially answered questions will give you more credit than two completed questions and two blank questions.

- Budget your time for each question.
  - 50% outlining
  - 50% writing

- Write your time estimates in the margin.

STEP 4: ☞ Reread the directions.

STEP 5: ☞ Reread the question and circle important words concerning what and how to write the answer (see *Essay Direction Words* on page 245).

STEP 6: ☞ Always organize your essay first by recreating your graphic organizer or outline.

STEP 7: ☞ Write methodically.

- Get involved with your answer—express your emotion.

- Leave a space between lines, if possible, so that you can add more information later if you choose; use appropriate left and right margins.

- Define any terms you use; do not use non-standard language or abbreviations.

- Use concrete examples.

- Introduction:
  - Begin by restating the question in your own words.
  - Establish tone and attitude.
  - Be sure all following sentences relate to the thesis.

- Use a good thesis statement that includes:
    - a specific subject
    - a specific condition, feeling, or your position on the topic
- Body:
    - Use transitional words or statements.
    - State main ideas clearly.
    - Reinforce these ideas with supporting details.
    - Support the details with examples whenever possible.
    - Be sure to stay on track with the topic—answer the question.

- Conclusion:
    - Use a summary sentence.
    - Restate the main idea and point of view, but do not use examples.
    - State how you proved, supported, or defended your original idea.
    - Give the reader a sense of conclusion.

STEP 8: ☞ Check your work.

- First, check for content.
    - Did you answer the key words directly and precisely?
    - Did you stick to your main point of view?
    - Did you include enough details to support a clear statement?

- Second, check for organization. (Everything should tie together closely.)
    - Introduction
    - Body
    - Conclusion

- Third, check for mechanics. Are there any:
  - Omitted words
  - Spelling errors
  - Grammatical errors
  - Punctuation errors
  - Awkward phrases
  - Transitional statements to move smoothly from one paragraph to another, such as *first, second, third, then, however, finally,* etc.

STEP 9: ☞ Be sure to express what you really mean to say.

- Be concise—don't ramble.

- Be certain to answer the question.

- Demonstrate relationships between/among main points.

- Include examples whenever possible and appropriate.

- If in doubt, let your answer be more general than specific. (e.g. "In the 1920s . . ." rather than "In 1923 . . .")

- Use the asterisk system to add additional information when enough space has not been left. However, avoid using this too many times.

STEP 10: ☞ If you run out of time, write "This is where I ran out of time" on your paper and include your outline.

STEP 11: ☞ What to do if you don't know the answer/topic:

- Look for "overlap" in what you do know.

- Look for ambiguous questions.

- Try to find relationships between what you studied and the question.

- Look through other parts of the test for clues.

©Incentive Publications, Inc., Nashville, TN

IF YOU ARE ASKED TO:	YOU SHOULD DO THE FOLLOWING:	EXAMPLES:
Analyze	Break down or separate a problem or situation into separate factors and/or relationships. Draw a conclusion, make a judgment, or make clear the relationship you see based on your breakdown.	Analyze the main story line in Chapter 2 and how it sets the stage for Chapter 3.
Categorize	Place items under headings already labeled by your teacher.	Categorize the items on the left under the proper headings on the right.
Classify	Place items in related groups; then name or title each group.	Listed below are 20 items. Classify them in 4 main groups; then name each group.
Compare	Tell how things are alike; use concrete examples.	Compare the American government system with that of the German government.
Contrast	Tell how things are different; use supporting concrete examples.	Contrast the writing styles of Shakespeare and Bacon.
Criticize	Make a judgment of the work of art or literature and support your opinion.	Criticize the use of cigarette advertising in magazines.
Deduce	Trace the course; derive a conclusion by reasoning.	Deduce the following logic problem to arrive at one of the conclusions listed below.
Defend	Give enough details to prove the statement.	Defend the statement "innocent until proven guilty."
Define	Give the meaning.	Define plankton.
Describe	Give an account in words; trace the outline or present a picture.	Describe Grand Coulee Dam.

From *Senior High Study Skills Booklet*, Jefferson County Schools, Colorado, © 1983. Used by permission.

ESSAY DIRECTION WORDS (continued)

IF YOU ARE ASKED TO:	YOU SHOULD DO THE FOLLOWING:	EXAMPLES:
Diagram	Use pictures, graphs, charts, mind maps, and flowcharts to show relationships of details to main ideas.	Diagram the offices of the federal government.
Discuss	Consider the various points of view by presenting all sides of the issue.	Discuss the use of chemotherapy in the treatment of cancer.
Distinguish	Tell how this is different from others similar to it.	Distinguish the three types of mold we have studied in class.
Enumerate	List all possible items.	Enumerate the presidents of the United States since Lincoln.
Evaluate	Make a judgment based on the evidence and support it; give the good and bad points.	Evaluate the use of pesticides.
Explain	Make clear and plain; give the reason or cause.	Explain how a natural disaster can help mankind.
Illustrate	Give examples, pictures, charts, diagrams, or concrete examples to clarify your answer.	Illustrate the use of a drawbridge.
Interpret	Express your thinking by giving the meaning as you see it.	Interpret the line "Water, water everywhere and not a drop to drink."
Justify	Give some evidence by supporting your statement with facts.	Justify the decision to bomb Nagasaki, Japan.
List	Write in a numbered fashion.	List five reasons to support your statement.
Outline	Use a specific and shortened form to organize main ideas supporting details and examples.	Outline the leading cause of World War II.

©Incentive Publications, Inc., Nashville, TN

From *Senior High Study Skills Booklet*,
Jefferson County Schools, Colorado, © 1983. Used by permission.

IF YOU ARE ASKED TO:	YOU SHOULD DO THE FOLLOWING:	EXAMPLES:
Paraphrase	Put in your own words.	Paraphrase the first paragraph of the Gettysburg Address.
Predict	Present solutions that could happen if certain variables were present.	Predict the ending of the short story written below.
Prove	Provide factual evidence to back up the truth of the statement.	Prove that the whaling industry has led to near-extinction of certain varieties of whales.
Relate	Show the relationship between concepts.	Relate man's survival instincts to those of animals.
Review	Examine the information critically. Analyze and comment on the important statements.	Review the effects of television advertisements on the public.
State	Establish by specifying. Write what you believe and back it with evidence.	State your beliefs in the democratic system of government.
Summarize	Condense the main points in the fewest words possible.	Summarize early man's methods of self-defense.
Synthesize	Combine parts or pieces of an idea, situation, or event.	Synthesize the events leading up to the Civil War.
Trace	Describe in steps the progression of something.	Trace the importance of the prairie schooner to the opening of the West.
Verify	Confirm or establish the truth of accuracy of point of view with supporting examples, evidence, and facts.	Verify the Declaration of Independence.

From *Senior High Study Skills Booklet*, Jefferson County Schools, Colorado, © 1983. Used by permission.

Introduction

- Clearly state the main points.

- Change the original question to a statement and include the main points.

- Create a good thesis statement.

Body

Each paragraph should include:
- transitional word or statement
- main ideas
- supporting details
- examples

(Be sure these points directly relate to the question and the topic in the introduction.)

Conclusion

- Begin with a good summary statement.

- Include the main points covered in the body but do not rewrite the body using different wording.

- State how you proved, supported, or defended your original intent in the introduction.

Open-Book Test Strategies

● Be prepared.
- Bring the following (be sure to clear all materials with the instructor before the date):
    ▲ Writing utensils (erasable ink pen, mechanical pencils with erasers)
    ▲ Plenty of paper (lined and unlined, scratch paper, graph paper, etc.)
    ▲ Texts, other references
    ▲ Text/class notes
    ▲ Handouts
    ▲ Lab reports
    ▲ Study sheets, outlines, graphic organizers
    ▲ 3″ x 5″ index cards/flash cards

● Know your textbook.
- Be very familiar with:
    ▲ Table of contents
    ▲ Index
    ▲ Special appendices
    ▲ Lists, charts, graphs, tables, summaries
    ▲ Author's intent in presentation of the material

● Read the chapters to be tested.
- Know the content.
- Know where to find associated information in other chapters.

- Make a special study guide several days in advance.
  - Anticipate test questions and group all associated information together with page numbers (color coding is very effective).
  - Save yourself valuable test-taking time by constructing:
    - ▲ Lists of vocabulary words (double-check the spelling), grouping according to topic
    - ▲ Brief graphic organizers or outlines for essay questions
    - ▲ Graphic organizers of major concepts with supporting ideas and examples
    - ▲ Your own concept index with page numbers from your notes and text (remember to number your notes and all other papers)
  - Use color coded flags or sticky notes to identify location of information (see *Test-Taking Tools* on page 219).

- When you get the test:
  - Scan the test quickly and look for a format (i.e., T/F, multiple-choice, fill-in-the-blank, matching, essay questions).
  - Plan your "attack" and organize your time appropriately:
    - ▲ Notice which sections are worth the most points.
    - ▲ Notice which sections seem to be related according to subject area.
    - ▲ Essay questions take more time—plan for this.
    - ▲ Read and then reread all directions carefully. Circle specific words necessary for answering the question (see *Essay Direction Words* on page 245).

Take-Home Test Strategies

- Take-home tests measure how well you research, organize, and combine information.

- Before you leave class:

  - Scan the entire test and ask any questions you might have.

  - Be sure that you understand all directions.

  - List all references/materials to be used. (When in doubt, ask the teacher.)

  - Be very clear about the due date, exact time, and teacher expectations.

  - Ask about any restrictions.

  - Find out the expected length for answers if essay questions are involved.

  - Find out the expected format for completing essay questions (handwritten, typed, etc.)

- At home: (see *Test-Taking Tools* on page 219)

STEP 1: ☞ Gather any/all needed materials.

- Textbook, additional references, handouts
- Text/class notes, reading notes, notes from outside assignments and research
- Dictionary/Thesaurus
- Computer
- Study sheets, 3" x 5" index cards, flash cards, graphic organizers or outlines
- Writing utensils
- Student handbook for writing tips

STEP 2: ☞ Plan your time allotment for each part of the test depending on point value—begin with the most valuable part.

STEP 3: ☞ Read the entire test.

- Read all directions very carefully.
- Look for related questions and answers throughout the test.
- Circle or flag qualifiers (words).
- Try to understand the overall objectives of the test and what the teacher wants from you.

STEP 4: ☞ Plan and organize your answers.

- Use this book to refer to specific test strategies in this section.
- Double-check all objective test answers.
- Be sure all essay answers are well-written. Use graphic organizers/outlines for initial organization.
- Make a list of the references you use and attach it to your test.
    1) Never copy directly from any source.
    2) If you do use quotations, be sure to use the proper punctuation and reference identification.
- Use the proper format for works cited page.

STEP 5: ☞ If you have time, write a first draft and then recopy it, proofreading for sentence structure, spelling, punctuation, content, accurate grammar, organization, and clarity.

STEP 6: ☞ Have several people proofread your work.

STEP 7: ☞ Staple all papers together before handing in the test.

STEP 8: ☞ Be sure your name is on every page of the test and pages are in correct order.

- Use a cover protector (plastic) if possible.

Watch What You're Doing!

LISTEN	for oral directions
LOOK	over the entire test
WRITE	brief notes; recreate graphic organizers
BUDGET	time to allow for completion
READ	directions twice; circle key words
ANSWER	all questions; flag unsure answers, then check later
CHECK	all answers

Review Your Returned Test

- Why?

    - To avoid repeated mistakes.

    - Know what a teacher wants on a test.

    - Review important feedback for future use.

- Read all of the grader's comments.

    - Do not become defensive.

    - Turn any criticism into a useful tool for future reference.

    - Learn from your mistakes—take a positive viewpoint.

    - Make a mental note of the positive comments and try to repeat these achievements.

- Look for specifics.

    - In what format was the test?

    - Note what types of questions you answer well.

    - Note what types of questions are your weakest; review test-taking strategies for these types of questions.

    - Was important information missing from your text/class notes, study sheets, or graphic organizer?

        ▲ Why was it missing?

        ▲ Was it recorded incorrectly?

        ▲ What can you do in the future to correct this?

    - Did you allow yourself enough time for each part of the test?

    - What amount of the test was covered in class notes, outside reading assignments, and class discussion periods? What was emphasized constantly?

- Pay attention to class discussion of the test.

    - Write notes on improvements you could have made.

    - Correct the wrong answers—write better answers.

    - Listen closely for teacher comments and how they might apply to future tests.

- Keep all tests in your home filing system (see *Hints for Getting Organized* on page 43).

If You Did Poorly On The Test

- Get Help From:

    - Teacher(s)

    - Family

    - Friends/other students in class that are doing well

    - Tutor(s), adults, or students who have taken the class before

    - Additional references: software, alternative textbooks, supportive classes

    - Study Groups

FOCUS ON

ETC.

1. Always be an active learner: Hear It, See It, Say It, Write It, and Do It.

2. Use your thinking skills effectively. Choose tools that will maximize your own individual learning style strengths and minimize your weaknesses.

3. Practice problem-solving and decision-making steps.

4. Be prepared for teacher conferences.

5. Utilize questioning skills to your advantage.

6. Apply a spelling system that really works.

7. Use and organize a plan of attack for independent study projects.

8. Apply divergent thinking characteristics to your learning.

9. Strive to use higher-level thinking skills to relate information.

10. Learn how to learn to make the most efficient use of your time.

BE AN ACTIVE LEARNER

Why Be an Active Learner?

To truly understand, transfer, apply, memorize, or recall information, you need to become an active participant in the learning process and physically do something with that information—not just let it remain on the paper and read it over and over again. For most of us, about the second time we read information written on a page, our mind has absorbed all that it is going to understand from that material. You need to do something else with that information in order to remember it longer.

Practice better learning strategies by applying all your senses to your study skills. By combining all of these forces you can better integrate the information into your brain and retain it more successfully.

Remember to do all of the following at the same time:

HEAR IT: Constantly talk aloud to yourself when studying. If you say it you will also hear it.

SEE IT: Look at the information at the same time you say it and hear it.

SAY IT: Repeat aloud the information at least three times before moving on to something new.

WRITE IT: Take reading text notes, write on 3" x 5" cards, make lists, etc. while talking out loud. This actively forces your mind to review it in a different way other than just rereading it.

DO IT: Use motion: walk or pace as you talk, act out the information, say it in front of a mirror. Create graphic organizers, flip through flash cards, etc.

Use these ideas to create active learning:

LEARNING STYLES
- Suggested Aids for Left/Right Brain Learners on page 21
- Suggested Aids for Learning Modalities on page 27

TIME MANAGEMENT AND ORGANIZATION SKILLS
- Organize Your Materials! on page 40
- The Wonders of Color Coding on page 46
- Take Control: Use a "To Do" List on page 53
- Use a Monthly Calendar on page 56
- Scheduling Your Study Time on page 62
- Appropriate Study Time Activities on page 68
- Study Time Warmup on page 70
- Study Smart Vocabulary on page 71

To develop successful thinking skills, you must gather information, take a new approach when necessary, and look at the whole picture from different angles. Thinking is a skill which can be improved with continual and deliberate effort. You have to *intend* to think through problem-solving strategies and open your mind to creativity.

These ideas will sharpen your thinking and increase your creative and decision making skills. Try some of them and you may be surprised by the wonderful results!

Learn to See the Whole Picture

- Break it down by looking at the details.
- Look for organized patterns in the material.
  - chronological order
  - cause/effect
  - comparison/difference
  - series
  - problem/solution
- Consider your surroundings and what is happening
- Consider your overall goal and the desired outcome

Be Flexible with Your Thinking

- Brainstorm as many solutions/answers as you can.
- Try an entirely new approach.
- Write your ideas so that you can refer to them from day-to-day.
- Spend some time with others who are trying to solve the problem.

Practice Making Decisions

- Like most everything else, it becomes easier the more you do it.
- Clarify and set your goals and think about what you want.
- Observe the situation carefully—try to see things you have never noticed.

Be Open to Change

- Try to have a positive mental attitude toward most changes.
- See the positive side and what you can do to improve it for yourself and others.
- Think of ways you can turn the negative aspects into positive aspects.
- Remember that thinking can be either wasted or improved.

Learn to Compare Pros and Cons of Change

- Fold a piece of paper in half vertically.
- Place a "+" on the top of the left column.
- Place a "−" on the top of the right column.
- When approaching any difficult problem-solving task or decision, write all of the positive and negative aspects, no matter how trivial or foolish they may seem to you.
- Compare the columns and THINK, then ACT.

A teacher is more than a person who stands in front of the classroom and imparts knowledge. How wonderful it would be for students if teachers could open up the tops of their students' heads and pour precious bits of ideas and details into every nook and cranny! But there is much more to teaching than that.

Teachers like to share what they have learned through books and experiences. They want their students to understand the concepts they teach. Throughout the learning experience, teachers not only encourage their students to apply what they have learned, but they motivate their students to reason, think, question, and relate the material to other information so that it makes sense.

It's good to focus your thoughts on what teachers try to do. It's so easy to overlook a teacher's good qualities when you're having trouble in his or her class and/or you personally do not like the teacher. If you stop to think about it, you definitely learn better from teachers you like and enjoy. But what about those instructors who share their course content in a way that is less than enjoyable to you? What can you do if you really do not like a teacher or find it difficult to relate to a teacher? Give yourself permission not to like the teacher; then turn all of your energy toward positive thoughts of learning the course content. Demonstrate respect and courtesy toward your teacher—your future success depends on your attitude and commitment toward making the best out of the situation. Just remember that teachers are people, too. Besides, if you can learn some important "people skills," life will be a lot easier for you!

STEP 1: ☞ **Face it—YOU have the problem.**

Even if you think it is entirely the other person's fault (the teacher), you have a problem because the "problem" bothers you. Take ownership of the problem.

STEP 2: ☞ **Try to identify the problem.**

Determine what it is that bothers or disturbs you. Is it really the *person* or what the person *does*? Is this problem enough of a priority for you to take up your time and energy? If you can see the problem for what it is, you can begin to look for the solution(s).

STEP 3: ☞ **Look at your options.**

You can continue to waste negative energy on the problem and let it interfere with learning, or you can give yourself permission to dislike (or even hate) the problem and then refocus your energies on a positive path. Walking down the "positive path" allows you to pick up what you need—you feel more at ease with yourself. Running down the "negative path" only serves to wear you down—you won't have the opportunity to pick up anything along the way. Say this to yourself: "I don't like this and that's OK. Now, what can I do to get what I want or need?" In other words, "I don't like this class/teacher and that's OK. Now, what can I do to learn the information and get the grade I want?"

STEP 4: ☞ **Think of several solutions.**

Be practical, realistic, and serious. Will these solutions really work? Can I give each solution an honest try? What are the consequences of each solution? What are the possible results of each solution? Write the solutions on a piece of paper, and, if time permits, give yourself time to think about them. Select your best two or three options. Dedicate yourself to putting one or more solutions into practice. Try each option, if necessary, before deciding on one.

STEP 5: ☞ **Put your solution(s) into practice.**

Begin with a positive attitude. You've thought through your solution(s) step-by-step and now you have enough self-confidence to start your "plan of attack." Think of it as a learning experience—you'll know so much if you should have to face this same problem in the future! If your approach to people is positive, your efforts will reflect positively on you. If your solution doesn't work to your satisfaction, try another solution—but don't quit! You have everything to gain and nothing to lose. Evaluate your decision, choice, and solution.

Suppose you have a problem (misunderstanding, lack of understanding, question, or need extra help) with a class or teacher and you don't know quite how to approach the teacher. It's really easier to solve than you might think. Follow these simple rules and you'll enjoy success!

1. Know what you want to ask or discuss before the conference. Write it on paper if necessary.

2. Rehearse your approach and questions/statements mentally and orally.

3. Find a time when the teacher is not busy with students or other teachers and is not in a hurry—a time when the teacher can devote some focused attention to your conversation is best. Set up an appointment if necessary.

4. Arrive a minute or two early or arrange to stay after class if necessary.

5. Begin with a positive statement and then simply state what you want or need. *Example:* "I'm sincerely interested in learning the information your class (lab, lecture, etc.) offers. But, lately I'm having a hard time understanding and keeping up, and I'd like to know what I can do to help myself."

6. Actively listen and take notes on what the teacher says and/or suggests. Thank the instructor for her time and assure her that you will try to put the suggestions into practice.

7. Tell the teacher that you will get in touch with him in two weeks (or the appropriate time) to share the improvements or to ask for further assistance.

8. Find ways to demonstrate your interest in class. Take part in discussions, ask thoughtful questions, and try to use some of the suggestions/ideas the teacher related to you during your conference, etc.

9. MOST OF ALL, be positive, courteous, considerate, willing to see the other side, and willing to try!

READING	WRITING	THINKING
determining purpose	fluency	recall/memory
determining rate	writing legibly	understanding concepts
effective note taking	spelling	visualization
recognizing signals	note taking	understanding organizational patterns
surveying material	clear, organized expression	critical thinking
developing a system	creativity	brainstorming
questioning	editing notes	classifying
reciting	proofreading	relaxation
reviewing	self-expression	
determining main ideas	reading	
intent to remember	creativity	
predicting	positive thinking	
reading charts	mindset of intentional learning	
comprehension	summarizing	
vocabulary development	relating and transferring concepts	
fluency	understanding relationships between main ideas and supporting details	
writing	evaluating	
	curiosity	

CLASSROOM SKILLS	PERSONAL ATTRIBUTES	TEST-TAKING SKILLS
active listening	curiosity	organizing information
note taking, writing	serious intent to learn	recognizing anxiety
speaking (relating ideas clearly)	patience	recall/memory
brainstorming	knowledge of learning style	practice
discussion skills	risk taking	overlearning
test-taking skills	thinking with an open mind	scheduling
completing homework	organizing	test-wiseness
organizing assignments and notebooks	prioritizing	organizing
classifying	willing to practice	positive attitude
locating information quickly	goal setting	concentrating
relating concepts	positive thinking	focusing thoughts
questioning	perseverance	
reading flexibility	understanding of confusion and boredom	
focusing concentration	flexibility	
demonstrating interest	realistic and constructive use of time	
showing respect		
patience		
understanding directions		
knowledge of self-commitment		
independence		

©Incentive Publications, Inc., Nashville, TN

Creative Problem-Solving Steps

1. Identify and describe the problem
2. Recognize and define the importance of the problem
3. Produce alternative solutions
4. Evaluate the alternative solutions
5. Develop and evaluate a plan

Divergent Thinking Characteristics

FLUENCY	ORIGINALITY	FLEXIBILITY	ELABORATION
• Generating ideas	• Unique ideas	• Changing ideas	• Expanding ideas
• Brainstorming	• Unusual qualities	• Brainstorming	• Adding details

Bloom's Taxonomy

(Levels of thinking from easiest to most difficult)

Knowledge = recall, recognition, factual answers
(label, list, memorize, name, define)

Comprehension = understand, summarize
(classify, judge, show, translate, explain, review)

Application = show knowledge, demonstrate
(predict, tell, identify, locate, organize, choose, illustrate)

Analysis = break down into parts, look at pieces
(distinguish, relate, classify, compare/contrast, examine)

Synthesis = combine new ideas, new ways
(create, make, solve, compose, imagine, develop, predict)

Evaluation = make judgments for criteria
(defend, argue, assess, evaluate)

Gardner's 8 Multiple Intelligences

VERBAL/LINGUISTIC DOMINANCE

Students strong in this type of intelligence have highly developed verbal skills, and often think in words. They do well on written assignments, enjoy reading, and are good at communicating and expressing themselves.

LOGICAL/MATHEMATICAL DOMINANCE

Students strong in this intelligence are able to think in abstractions and can handle complex concepts. They readily see patterns or relationships in ideas. They like to work with numbers and perform mathematical operations, and they approach problem-solving exercises with the tools of logic and rational thought.

VISUAL/SPATIAL DOMINANCE

Students with this dominant intelligence think in images, symbols, colors, pictures, patterns, and shapes. They like to perform tasks that require "seeing with the mind's eye"—tasks that require them to visualize, imagine, pretend, or form images.

BODY/KINESTHETIC DOMINANCE

Students dominant in this intelligence have strong body awareness and a sharp sense of physical movement. They communicate best through body language, physical gestures, hands-on activities, active demonstrations, and performance tasks.

MUSICAL/RHYTHMIC DOMINANCE

Students with this dominant intelligence enjoy music, sounds, rhythmic patterns, and variations in tones or rhythms. They enjoy listening to music, composing music, interpreting music, performing to music, and learning with music playing in the background.

INTRAPERSONAL DOMINANCE

Students with this dominant intelligence prefer to work alone because they are self-reflective, self-motivated, and in tune with their own feelings, beliefs, strengths, and thought processes. They respond to intrinsic rather than extrinsic rewards and may demonstrate great wisdom and insight when presented with personal challenges and independent study opportunities.

INTERPERSONAL DOMINANCE

Students with this dominant intelligence have a keen understanding of other people. They are adept at establishing meaningful peer relationships, have an ability to empathize with others, show good teamwork skills, and frequently act as peacemakers or moderators.

NATURALISTIC DOMINANCE

Howard Gardner defines a naturalist as a person who recognizes flora and fauna plus other consequential distinctions in the natural world and uses the ability productively. A naturalist demonstrates the ability to understand patterns, relationships, and connections in nature.

Questions that Foster Philosophical Thinking

- Why?
- If that is so, what follows?
- How do you know that?
- Is this your point?
- What is your reason for saying that?
- Is it possible that . . . ?
- Are there other ways of . . . ?
- How else could you view this matter?

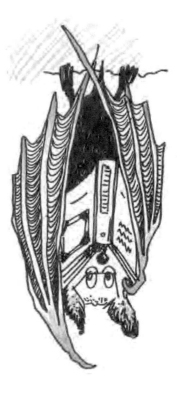

Good Study/Review Questions

- Can you briefly summarize what you just read? What/ Who was important and why?
- Can you explain your answer?
- Can you state examples and tell why they are important?
- Do you agree? Why or why not?
- How did you arrive at your answer or solution? What are your "thinking" steps?
- What facts support your view and can you think of others not stated?
- Can you apply these ideas to other situations or information?
- Can you add information to this subject or compare and contrast it with what you already know?

Steps in Answering a Question

STEP 1 ☞ **Read**
- Read the question carefully.
- What is the question asking you?
- Do you know the meaning of all the words?
- Underline the key words.

STEP 2 ☞ **Decide**
Determine if it is a factual or thought question.

STEP 3 ☞ **Locate**
Find information relating to the question.
Write the information in your own words.

STEP 4 ☞ **Organize**
Does your answer make sense? Does it answer the question?

In Order to Learn Anything

- Link it with something you already know about the subject. *Ask yourself:* "What do I already know about this topic or subject?"

- Understand why the information is important and how you can use it in the future. *Ask yourself:* "Why is this important information to hear? How can I use this in the future?"

- Review how you have tried to learn in the past and possible strategies of learning the information. *Ask yourself:* "How have I tried to learn this already? What do I need to change to learn this?"

- Organize the information into logical patterns or groups. *Ask yourself:* "Can I identify the main topics, sub-topics, details, and examples? How do these relate to each other?"

- Break down the information into smaller groups and relate main topics with details. *Ask yourself:* "How can I divide this material into smaller units for easier learning? How can I divide this material into some main topic areas and then link the details to each topic?"

- Teach it to someone. *Ask yourself:* "Can I show someone a system or strategy to learn this material? Can I create and use a graphic organizer or mnemonic device?"

What Anyone Needs to Do to Think

- Communicate information with/to someone else through writing or conversation.
- Experiment and initiate ideas.
- Constantly review, evaluate, and analyze the information.
- Conceptualize and link new ideas/information with old ideas/information.
- Interpret information through inductive and deductive thinking.
- Exercise flexible thinking.
- Use problem-solving processes.
- Apply known facts.

Things that Affect Attention

- Your mood/attitude
- Physical and mental state
- Stress
- Your ability to pace yourself
- Your ability to control impulses
- Your ability to control distractions
- Amount of material to learn and intended pace of learning
- Your goal and understanding of your commitment

Stress can be either a motivating or a demotivating factor. Good stress helps you succeed at accomplishing a specific project or task and leaves when you have completed the project or task. Bad stress inhibits your productivity and accomplishments and causes negative effects mentally and physically. It does not leave when the project is done or the task is completed.

Often, you can control whether stress will be good or bad. Bad stress often plays a negative part in your learning and in your life in general. Much of stress reduction includes good time management and organizational skills so that you can successfully and productively accomplish your goal and give yourself the gift of extra time. Quality—not quantity—is the key.

Check out the following "stress buster" ideas. Use them to improve on what you are already doing and try some new ones!

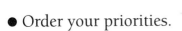

- Order your priorities.
  - Decide what is worth your time and effort and what is not.
  - Rank items according to true priorities.
  - List things that are stressful, and things that are relaxing.
  - Decide what can be changed, combined, and/or eliminated, and what is necessary.
  - Assign appropriate amounts of time to each, and rank each according to time of day.
  - Be sure to reward yourself whenever appropriate and possible.

- Set and track your goals carefully.
  - Constantly make a "reality check" with your goals. Are they realistic? Are they necessary? Can you accomplish them to your satisfaction? Don't cause yourself extra stress by sticking to outdated/unnecessary goals—change them whenever appropriate.

- ■ Always connect your goals to your daily schedule.
- ■ Try to resolve any conflict when others' goals do not match yours ASAP.
- ■ Track your goals on a daily basis; continual positive feedback is essential.

- ● Get appropriate sleep.
  - ■ Try to keep a fairly regular schedule.

- ● Plan your day.
  - ■ Take 10 minutes at the beginning of each day to review your schedule/calendar and create a "To Do" list (see page 53).

- ● Use a calendar.
  - ■ Break down large jobs into smaller ones and set due dates for each deadline.

- ● Use an assignment book/daytimer.

- ■ You are 10 times more likely to do or remember something if you write it down than if you do not.
- ■ It takes less time to write it down and occasionally review it then it does to worry about forgetting it because you did not write it down.

- ● Use a bulletin board/dry-erase board.
  - ■ Posting information is a great reminder.
  - ■ This gives you a specific place for notes, calendars, etc. so you won't worry about misplacing them.

- ● Use "stickie" notepads.
  - ■ The convenience of placing them anywhere and everywhere will consistently remind you of tasks to be done and you won't have to worry about forgetting things.

- ● Avoid distractions.
  - ■ Use an answering machine or have someone answer the phone when you study; this cuts down on your frustration when you have to refocus your thoughts if you are interrupted.
  - ■ Turn your attention to completing your goals during each session, and tune out inappropriate and confusing thoughts.

- Organize your workspace to maximize your time and control distractions.
  - Purchase useful organizing items that will keep materials organized (drawer divider trays, paper trays, color-coded file folders, etc.).
  - Avoid placing any distracting items on the top of your desk.
  - Throw out things you do not use; don't be continually frustrated by "wading through" unnecessary items every time you need something.

- Create an organizational system that really works for you.
  - Experiment and change any stressful aspects as soon as you notice any frustration with them; make it a point to be flexible and patient with yourself.
  - Make sure your system is easy and comfortable for you.

- Use a watch/clock to your advantage.
  - Give yourself extra time to accomplish things or get somewhere; automatically build an appropriate amount of time into your schedule so you won't worry about it.
  - Try being somewhere 5–10 minutes early or completing an assignment a day or two early; let yourself experience how good it really feels.
  - Always estimate how long it will take you to accomplish an assignment or task before you begin.

- Make "To Do" lists (see page 53).
  - Don't spend time worrying about forgetting to do something when you can short circuit that frustration by simply writing it down.
  - Prioritizing tasks and assigning them to an appropriate time of day will more likely insure success.

- Combine activities whenever possible.
  - Use your time and energy to avoid stress rather than add to it.
  - Always ask yourself: "How can I do this activity/assignment, these errands/jobs, to avoid stress?"
  - Quickly identify any hidden shortcuts in any project.

- Practice saying NO.
  - To activities or tasks you really don't need to do, or things you don't have time to accomplish to your satisfaction.
  - Consider your physical and emotional energy level before saying yes.

- Find the best time to do things.
  - Know and use your best time of day for study time (when your concentration and learning power is at its best); work with yourself, not against yourself.

- Set a schedule and keep it.
  - Realistically recognize "controllable" and "uncontrollable" time to schedule yourself (you cannot control every situation every time).
  - Be selective; don't commit yourself to things you don't have the resources to successfully complete; always ask yourself, "Is this realistic?"
  - Be flexible; don't create unnecessary stress, be creative and make the time to sit down and figure out why your schedule is or is not working for you.

- Always try to dramatically increase your focused, productive time.
  - Strive to learn to do more in less time and give yourself more free time.

- Anticipate problems and plan effective strategies to avoid them.

- Don't procrastinate: Just do it!

- Seriously assess your use of time every week.
  - Identify and eliminate unnecessarily stressful situations.

- Develop "signals" that let people know when you're working and don't want to be disturbed.
  - Post a "Do Not Disturb: Studying" sign on the door.
  - Clearly share your study time hours with your family/peers and then stick to it.

- Build and maintain positive relationships.
  - Make the time to develop positive relationships.
  - Be sensitive and flexible to others' needs (their space, time, etc.).
  - When appropriate and realistic, avoid people who cause you negative emotions and stress.
  - When you can't—quickly give yourself permission not to like the situation/people involved and then make a conscious decision to lower your stress level with whatever positive action you can take at the time.
  - Balance your goals, personal values, priorities, family needs/activities, and friends/social activities. It takes less time and energy to be proactive and positive than reactive and negative.

- Laugh
  - The average person laughs 15 times a day. How do you compare?
  - Laughter has been shown to:
    - ▲ Reduce stress
    - ▲ Relax muscles
    - ▲ Release your body's natural pain killers
    - ▲ Increase mental alertness, attention span, and sensory perception
    - ▲ Increase cooperation and productivity
    - ▲ Boost the immune system
- Connect with nature
  - Spend five minutes each day watching an aquarium, observing animals, looking out a window.
- Use meditation/practiced relaxation techniques
  - Let your mind wander to a place where it can relax
  - Have someone rub your shoulders, neck, and feet
  - Choose an object to focus on to intentionally relax
  - Learn bio-feedback techniques
  - Think positive thoughts
  - Make relaxation a regular part of your daily schedule
- Eat right
- Enjoy music to relax
  - Avoid it while studying.
- Make time for hobbies you enjoy
- Exercise regularly
- Take a bath or shower
- Become aware of "stressors"
  - They can be happy or unhappy
  - Observe how you handle both types, and what effect this has on you

- Seek out quiet environments when appropriate at least once a day
- Take deep breaths when you first notice yourself becoming stressed
- Tell yourself tomorrow will be even better!

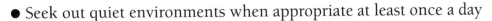

SUPER SPELLING SYSTEM

When using this system, divide your spelling list into small groups of three words. Work with only one group at a time.

STEP 1 ☞ **Study the words for two to three minutes**

- Concentrate—focus on each word for
  - ▲ Double letters (bookkeeper)
  - ▲ Words within words (tremendous)
  - ▲ Letter patterns (interpret)
  - ▲ Compounds (motherhood)
  - ▲ Number of syllables
  - ▲ Prefixes, suffixes (in-/im- beginnings, -able/-ible endings, -er/-or endings)
  - ▲ Exceptions to spelling rules
- Make quick mental pictures
- Think of nonsense sayings
- Pronounce it aloud three times
- Review and apply appropriate spelling rules (see *Spelling Rules* on page 280-281)

STEP 2 ☞ **Take a trial test**

- Have someone say the word to you, then use it in a sentence
- Write the word (do not spell it orally because that is not the way you will have to spell the word for the test)

STEP 3 ☞ **Correct the trial test**

- Say the word
- Have the person spell the word while you write it beside your spelling
- Check the two words for a match

STEP 4 ☞ **Rewrite the incorrect words**

- As you write, orally repeat each letter
- Remember to: **Hear it, See it, Say it, Write it, Do it** all at the same time

STEP 5 ☞ **Write all of the words on one 3" x 5" card**

- Place an asterisk by the words you have misspelled

STEP 6 ☞ **Retake the trial test**

- Correct yourself by checking the words against the 3" x 5" card
- Orally spell each word as you check the card
- Rewrite correctly, again, any incorrect words

STEP 7 ☞ **Post 3" x 5" cards where they can be seen every day, places such as**

- Your room, bulletin board, mirror, etc. (in upper left corner)
- Locker door at school
- Refrigerator door
- Binder
- Pocket (standing in the lunch line or when waiting for class to begin)
- For particularly difficult words, write each word on a separate 3" x 5" card

$\int$PELLING RULES

The rules listed below are some of the most commonly used for the English language. There are specific exceptions to almost every rule. It is not a complete list, however, so check your reference handbook for further help if needed. When in doubt (or it just doesn't "look right"), always look it up in a dictionary.

- **ie / ei**
    "I before E _except_ after C, or when it sounds like A, as in _neighbor_ or _weigh_"
    - ▲ most words are "ie"
    - ▲ when _not_ pronounced like a long "E" (ee), it most often is spelled "ei" (ex. neighbor, weigh, beige, eight)
    - ▲ when used after C write "ei" (ex. receipt, ceiling, receive)

- **er / or / ar / ur endings**
    - ■ most words end in "-er"

	Exceptions	
"or"	**"ar"**	**"ur"**
ambassador, bachelor, calculator, debtor, elevator, endeavor, governor, honor, humor, liquor, mayor, mirror, operator, professor, refrigerator, splendor, sponsor, visitor	beggar, burglar, familiar, grammar, nuclear	chauffeur, connoisseur, entrepreneur

- **Silent "e" endings (Suffix)**
    - ■ drop the "e" when the suffix begins with a vowel (ex. prime/primary, serve/service, like/liking
    - ■ do not drop the "e" when the suffix begins with a consonant (ex. nine/ninety, care/careless, peace/peaceful)

- **"y" endings (Suffix)**
  - vowel + "y" word = make no changes (ex. buy/buyer, joy/joyous)
  - consonant + "y" word = change "y" to "i"
    and add the suffix (ex. city/citified, fry/fried, lady/ladies)

- **Doubling final letters**
  - one syllable word + one vowel + one consonant = double final letter
    before adding suffix (ex. pan/panned, stop/stopped)
  - multi-syllable word + one vowel + one consonant (accent on
    last syllable + suffix begins with vowel) = double final letter
    before adding suffix (ex. forbid/forbidding, begin/beginning)
  - Exceptions are words ending in "x" and "w"
    (ex. box/boxed, tow/towing)

- **Plurals** (from one noun to more than one noun)
  - simply add "s" to most nouns
  - sh, ch, x, s, z ending = noun + "es" (ex. box/boxes)
  - consonant + "o" ending = add es (ex. tomato/tomatoes)
  - vowel + "o" ending = add s (ex. rodeo/rodeos)
  - all musical terms ending in "o" = add s (ex. cello/cellos)
  - "ful" endings = add "s" (exception: beware of the usage in the sentence; there is a
    difference between two teaspoons full and two teaspoonfuls)
  - "f" endings = how it is pronounced in its plural form dictates the spelling:
    hear the "f" = add "s" (ex. roof/roofs)
    hear the "v" = change "f" to "v" and add es (ex. wolf/wolves)
  - compound nouns (hyphenated or words in a phrase) = add "s" or "es" to the
    main word (ex. matrons of honor, sisters-in-law, heads of state, courts martial)

Some Special Exceptions that totally change or have more than one accepted spelling:

American	British	singular	plural
flavor	flavour	radius	radii
kilogram	kilogramme	child	children
theater	theatre	die	dice
wagon	waggon		
medieval	mediaeval		

SOME TIPS FOR PARENTS: HOW TO HELP AT HOME

It's your right and responsibility as a parent to set consistent, fair, realistic, and appropriate rules for your child. You can support and empower your student to become a successful independent learner by using these suggestions.

- Set high (but reasonable) expectations.

- Help them recognize and set realistic goals.

- Teach your child how to successfully cope with stress.

- Control how many total activities your child is involved in both in and out of school. Overcommitment leads to major stress.

- Make a point to talk with (not at) your child about daily activities. When appropriate, ask questions that foster higher-level thinking, not only questions that may be answered with "yes" or "no".

- Make positive comments and compliments to your child every day.

- Criticize constructively. Give frequent feedback.

- Encourage "hands-on" activities: kitchen chemistry, math puzzles, interactive computer/board games, etc.

- Identify and feed current "passions." Take your child to the library, museum, or to community activities of interest, etc.

- Help your child establish good time management techniques and check on this from time to time.

- Respect their study time. Help make it positive, efficient, and effective.

- Encourage your child to learn how to learn. Refer to this book often as a resource for great study skills and problem-solving strategies.

- Discuss your child's intent to learn with him. What are your child's goals now, a year from now, five years from now?

- Know how you and your child learn best and take advantage of this information. Apply effective learning strategies for individual learning styles.

- Put a priority on reading and demonstrate it! Read to them and read for yourself.

- Encourage good speaking and listening skills. Involve writing as much as possible.

- Monitor the appropriate use of TV, video/computer games, and telephone.

- Provide an adequate breakfast, lunch, and dinner for your child.

- Eat dinner together. Use this pleasant time to catch up on the day's events NOT to drill for answers, lecture them, etc.

- Talk about teachers in a positive tone in front of your child.

- Encourage your child to participate in the "extras" the school offers. Try one or two activities at a time.

- Know what classes and assignments your child has.

- Become familiar with their daily school schedules and classroom policies (late homework/make-up).

- Check school calendars for upcoming events, projects, meetings, etc. Be aware of activities by reading newsletters.

- Show your enthusiasm for education by taking an active interest in your child's schooling. Send notes to teachers, attend school functions, and volunteer/visit frequently.

- Find out when/if teachers are available for extra help.

- Have a conference with your child's teacher as appropriate and attend regularly scheduled parent/teacher conferences.

HELP! MY CHILD WON'T STUDY!

It may help to know you are not alone in facing this problem! No matter how much you—as a parent—want your child to succeed in school, children must learn for themselves self-discipline and the great benefits of making good decisions. This is an ongoing learning experience from a young age until they leave home. They will use these values throughout their lives. So start now—it's never too late!

Approach your child with the positive statement: "YOU have much control in deciding what activities you do. If YOU choose to demonstrate a consistent habit of studying without reminders, YOU also choose to do other activities. If YOU choose not to study and to have poor grades, then YOU choose not to do these activities."

Explain that every decision has a positive or negative consequence. Deciding to study and get good grades is just as much a conscious and deliberate choice as deciding not to study. By demonstrating (not just saying or promising) a consistent habit of studying (not just for a few days or weeks), your child also chooses to participate in school, family, and friend activities.

As a parent, you have the right and responsibility to enforce these decisions. Your student needs to see you in the positive role as a parent providing support and loving guidance to them. Enforce the "no studying = no activities" rule by reminding them that when they made the decision not to study on Wednesday (this week, etc.), they made the decision not to play with friends after school, go to the movie today, or play computer games.

It is more effective to wait until the activity is at hand than to remind or threaten, ". . . if you don't study now, there will be no playing with friends, computer games, movie." It makes a more lasting impression on them to wait until the time they want something to remind them of their earlier decisions that resulted in this negative result. Actions are more effective than words a great deal of the time.

Remember to be consistent, not to nag or remind them, and that in this area your role model as a parent is more important than your model as a friend. As a parent you have to do what's right, not what's easy!

STEP 1: ☞ **SELECT A TOPIC**

- Look through books and resource materials.
- Brainstorm for ideas with family and friends.
- Follow your own interests or hobbies.
- Interview others.
- Read the newspaper or a current magazine.
- Watch the news on TV.

STEP 2: ☞ **NARROW THE TOPIC**

- Limit the topic and consider the following: desired length, amount of in-class and out-of-class time needed, your access to resources, your time schedule.
- Narrow the topic enough so that you may cover it thoroughly, but not so much that there won't be enough available information.
- Form definite questions you want to answer. Avoid yes/no, one-word and short-phrase answers.

STEP 3: ☞ **PUT YOUR TOPIC TO THE TEST**

- How much information can you actually locate to answer the questions?
- Is the material easy to find in the media center, from resource people, etc? Can you take the material home?
- Can you complete the project by the due date?

STEP 4: ☞ **CHOOSE YOUR RESOURCES**

- Books, pamphlets, magazines
- TV, films, filmstrips, videotapes, movies
- People (interviews, polls, questionnaires)
- Travel
- Illustrated graphics (charts, graphs, tables, pictures)
- Experiment—use your senses.

STEP 5: ☞ **SCHEDULE YOUR TIME**

- Divide your time into realistic blocks. Consider the following:
  - → library/media center check-out time periods
  - → postal service (if you're sending for material)
  - → actual contact time with people (and time to make arrangements)
  - → in-class and homework time
  - → basic outline, rough draft, illustrations, front cover, and other steps in organizing the report/project

STEP 6: ☞ BEGIN YOUR RESEARCH

- Begin at the media center. Look for information related to your topic in the following areas:
  - → card catalog
  - → Reader's Guide
  - → reference section
  - → almanacs, maps
  - → visual center (filmstrips, cassettes, tapes, films, etc.)
- Keep a "running list" of titles, authors, publishers, and page numbers of every source you use (also note the call number or location beside each item).
- Skim through the material before writing anything. This saves time and energy.
- Stay organized.
  - → Keep everything related to the project in a notebook, box, filing card system, etc.
  - → Organize a notebook and section off the different aspects of the topic/report.
- Ask the librarian or your teacher any questions concerning resources (the media specialist might know a resource you overlooked).
- The more variety of materials you can collect, the better (if they are appropriate to the project).

STEP 7: ☞ ORGANIZE AND PRESENT YOUR PROJECT

- Be creative. Think of unusual ways to present your material/information (when the assignment allows it) such as:
  - → Slide shows
  - → Live interviews
  - → News broadcasts
  - → Videotapes
  - → Radio programs
  - → Computer graphics
  - → Pamphlets or brochures
  - → Murals
  - → Puppet plays
  - → Inventions with explanations
  - → Puzzles or games (involve other students)
  - → Three-dimensional models or exhibits
  - → Oral presentations (dress in costume)
  - → Speeches or testimonials (dress in costume)
- Be sure to:
  - → Rehearse before you give the presentation.
  - → Check all of the materials for proper order.
  - → Complete the assignment a day or so before it is due to allow for the addition of any last minute details and to let yourself relax.
  - → Recheck the original assignment to make sure your project/report satisfies all of the conditions or answers all of the questions and criteria.

CKNOWLEDGEMENTS

CMU Junior League. "Time Management" (page 34),
    "What To Do If You Missed An Assignment" (page 52): from
    The Campus Cache: A Cookbook For Study Skills, © 1982
    by Cherry Creek School District. Reprinted by permission.

Isakson, Peggy. "Power Reading System" (pages 158–161).
    Reprinted by permission.

Piccolo, JoAnne. Enumerative, Sequence, Cause-Effect,
    Comparison-Contrast, & Description Graphic Organizers
    (pages 137–141). Reprinted by permission.

Jefferson County Schools, Colorado. "Study Habits Inventory"
    (pages 36–38), "Surveying The Textbook" (pages 155–156),
    "Essay Direction Words" (pages 245–247): adapted from
    Senior High Study Skills Booklet, © 1983.
    Reprinted by permission.